The
ART
– of –
Trust
Building

The
ART
– of –
Trust
Building

Transform Lives, Teams, and Organizations

Dennis Reina, PhD,
and Michelle Reina, PhD

Berrett-Koehler
PUBLISHERS

Berrett-Koehler Publishers, Inc.
1333 Broadway, Suite P100
Oakland, CA 94612-1921
(510) 817-2277
bkconnection.com

ORDERING INFORMATION
Quantity sales. Special discounts are available on quantity purchases by corporations, associations, and others. For details, please go to bkconnection.com to see our bulk discounts or contact bookorders@bkpub.com for more information.
Individual sales. Berrett-Koehler publications are available through most bookstores. They can also be ordered directly from Berrett-Koehler: (800) 929-2929; bkconnection.com.
Orders for college textbook/course adoption use. Please contact Berrett-Koehler: (800) 929-2929.

Distributed to the US trade and internationally by Penguin Random House Publisher Services.

The authorized representative in the EU for product safety and compliance is
EU Compliance Partner, Pärnu mnt. 139b-14, 11317 Tallinn, Estonia,
www.eucompliancepartner.com, +372 5368 65 02.

Berrett-Koehler and the BK logo are registered trademarks of Berrett-Koehler Publishers, Inc.

Printed in the United States of America.

Berrett-Koehler books are printed on long-lasting acid-free paper. When it is available, we choose paper that has been manufactured by environmentally responsible processes. These may include using trees grown in sustainable forests, incorporating recycled paper, minimizing chlorine in bleaching, or recycling the energy produced at the paper mill.

Library of Congress Cataloging-in-Publication Data
Names: Reina, Dennis S., 1950- author | Reina, Michelle L., 1958- author
Title: The art of trust building : transform lives, teams, and organizations / Dennis Reina, PhD and
    Michelle Reina, PhD.
Description: First edition. | Oakland, CA : Berrett-Koehler Publishers, Inc, [2026] | Includes
    bibliographical references and index.
Identifiers: LCCN 2025024230 (print) | LCCN 2025024231 (ebook) | ISBN 9798890571458
    paperback | ISBN 9798890571465 pdf | ISBN 9798890571472 epub
Subjects: LCSH: Organizational behavior | Trust | Organizational effectiveness | Work environment
    | Psychology, Industrial
Classification: LCC HD58.7 .R4386 2026 (print) | LCC HD58.7 (ebook)
LC record available at https://lccn.loc.gov/2025024230
LC ebook record available at https://lccn.loc.gov/2025024231

First Edition
33 32 31 30 29 28 27 26 25   10 9 8 7 6 5 4 3 2 1

Book production: Happenstance Type-O-Rama
Cover design: Ashley Ingram

To our grandchildren, Henry and Phoebe,
who explore the world with wonderment
and trust, and remind us to do the same

Contents

Preface

Trust is at the heart of every strong relationship, team, and organization—no matter the size, industry, or location. And yet, in today's world, where social media noise, political division, and echo chambers dominate, trust is taking a serious hit. It has not lost its value—far from it. Trust is more essential than ever. But in a world clouded by noise, division, and disconnection, many are losing sight of just how vital trust truly is.

We see the effects everywhere: increased skepticism, fractured relationships, and a breakdown in meaningful collaboration.

So, here is the real question: How can we expect our society to thrive if trust isn't at the core of our relationships, businesses, and everyday interactions?

The truth is simple—even if it is hard to face: *we can't.*

Trust is not something that exists on its own—it's not passive nor static. It can be earned, lost, and rebuilt—but only through intentional, deliberate, courageous actions. Trust evolves, adapts, and requires ongoing care because it doesn't just happen. It doesn't simply show up—instead, it must actively be earned, consistently nurtured, and deliberately cultivated. The real challenge isn't deciding whether trust matters; it's learning how to create and sustain it. And that begins with you.

This is where *The Art of Trust Building* comes in to guide you. It is an intentional framework designed to take trust from a vague ideal and turn it into how you live, breathe, and practice every day. Trust building is a journey, and every great journey requires a proper set of tools to help you navigate toward the relationships, outcomes, and impact you and your team most want to create.

At our core, we all long for the same things—to trust and be trusted, to love and be loved, to care for our families, and to live meaningful, connected lives. Trust is the bridge that makes all of this possible. When trust is strong, relationships flourish, teams thrive, and what we achieve together often goes beyond what we imagined.

Here's the bottom line: to earn trust, we must be willing to give it.

Whether you're a team member, a leader, a parent, or a friend, this book is for you. It's meant to empower you with practical tools to take proactive, nurturing measures through powerful language, meaningful conversations, intentional behaviors—and gratitude— that build and strengthen trust in every part of your life.

When you master *The Art of Trust Building*, you gain an advantage across all avenues of your life, career, and business. People will seek your advice, leadership, and partnership. You will become the embodiment of what's possible when trust becomes the cornerstone of your way of being.

This book also offers a shared language for trust—a way to connect more authentically, lead more effectively, and build strong bonds across every area of your life.

We are on this journey with you.

Our focus on trust began when leaders kept coming to us, asking why change efforts were stalling, teams were struggling to collaborate, and key initiatives were falling short. We listened. We dug in. As we talked with people across all levels of organizations and reviewed assessment data, a clear pattern emerged—at the root of these issues was a lack of trust. That realization pushed us to dig deeper. We gained insight through our respective doctoral research yet felt a strong drive to better understand the dynamics of trust. Over the next four years, following our doctoral studies in the midnineties, we interviewed 378 leaders, held focus groups with hundreds of people, and worked with 67 organizations across 19 industries to uncover what really makes trust thrive—or break down.[1]

Over the next three decades, we have had the privilege to continue our research, to serve thousands of individuals and hundreds of organizations around the world, and respond to the growing need for trust. What began as a curiosity and research interest has become our life's work: supporting people to build and rebuild trust with practical tools that foster it, sustain it, and make it part of their everyday lives—at work and at home.

What you will ultimately unearth in these pages is a road map to expand your awareness of the creative and collaborative possibilities that exist in trusted relationships. You will do this by learning how to cultivate trust in every area of your life through concrete actions and tangible behaviors designed to build and sustain lasting relationships.

We've learned that everyone needs a starting point.

To get the most out of this book, we invite you to take the **Reina Individual Trust Assessment**.[2] It's a quick, powerful

way to see where you currently stand with trust in your relationships—how you build it, and where there are opportunities
to grow. Think of it as your personal starting point for deeper
insight and lasting change. Just head to the following link to begin:
reinatrustbuilding.com/ITS-book

Your journey to deeper trust and stronger relationships starts
here.

> *Dennis Reina, PhD*
> *Michelle Reina, PhD*
> Stowe, Vermont, USA
> September 2025

Introduction

The Trust Advantage:
How to Earn It and Keep It

Our trust building journey began more than thirty-five years ago.

While we were working with organizations to implement strategic initiatives, leaders frequently turned to us to help them understand why their efforts to lead change, develop teams, foster collaboration, and engender engagement were failing to produce results. Through many discussions, we discovered that trust—*and its breakdown*—was at the heart of these challenges—challenges that continue to confront organizations around the world today.

Throughout these decades, our personal and professional journey into trust building has been shaped by significant trials, tribulations, and triumphs. Together, we've faced four bouts of cancer, the loss of loved ones, and life-threatening medical crises. We've made sacrifices to pursue doctorates, raise a family, build a consulting firm, and write books—all while navigating the highs of business success and the setbacks of betrayals by those we trusted and, in some cases, *loved*.

These experiences taught us that trust fuels energy, confidence, and growth, while its absence depletes and destabilizes relationships, teams, and organizations.

We have come to understand that trust cannot be explored without acknowledging the hurt, disappointment, and breaches that come with the territory of relationships and of life itself. This understanding makes rebuilding trust not an option but an essential part of the process for individuals, teams, and organizations to grow stronger through the challenges trust presents.

The Trust Building Mindset

Imagine stepping into a meeting where everyone is operating within the shared belief that *"anything is possible."* You can feel the energy, the can-do attitude, the shared drive to create and collaborate.

This *is* the power of trust building when it's present.

Trust elevates energy, inspires confidence, nourishes the spirit, and opens the doors of innovation. The totality of this collective field of energy encourages people to dream bigger, take smarter risks, and sense that together, they're on the edge of something extraordinary.

But when trust is missing, doubt creeps in, suddenly—out of seemingly nowhere—suspicion sets in, communication breaks down, and even the simplest of tasks feels heavy. People shut down, retreat into silos, and start questioning each other—and themselves. This stark contrast makes one thing clear: *trust is the bridge between the business need for results and the human need for connection.*

So, where does trust begin?

Trust begins with you. It starts with your capacity for trust—your readiness and willingness to trust yourself and others. This inner capacity influences your thoughts, attitudes, and beliefs. It

colors your outlook—how open you are to new ideas, how willing you are to risk connection, how bravely you step into the
unknown.

When you trust yourself, you're more willing to lean into life's
gray areas—to move beyond rigid black-and-white thinking and
embrace complexity with curiosity. You become more open to
diverse perspectives, to differences, to dialogue.

Self-trust is what enables you to extend grace. To take a breath
before judging. To believe in the potential of others, even when
certainty isn't guaranteed. It's not about trusting unquestioningly.
It's about trusting consciously rooted in awareness, aligned with
your values, and fueled by the courage to grow.

Trust begins with your commitment to relationships.

But here's the truth—trust building isn't something you sit
back and wait for. When it comes to trust, you can't be on the
sidelines, hoping someone else takes the first step. With laser-like
focus, you've got to align your attitude, intention, and behavior to
an outcome that benefits everyone involved. When you do, trust
building becomes a way of being—something you practice and
carry with you and live every day as an expression of who you are.

Sounds simple, right? But it's not always easy.

We all want and need trust—and more and more people
recognize how valuable it is. What's less understood is that just
wanting or valuing trust isn't enough. Trust is earned through one
thing and one thing only, *your behavior.*

Through our years of research and practice, we developed
the Three Dimensions of Trust—a practical behavioral blueprint
to help you build trust with the people you work with, live with,
and love.

The Three Dimensions of Trust: A Behavioral Blueprint

Trust is inherently reciprocal: it grows when we give it, not just when we seek it. Likewise, when we take it for granted and abuse it, it withers and falls away. Built step by step over time, trust is nourished through mutual commitment and shared intention. The more we choose to give it to others and ourselves, the more it takes root and expands.

Yet, for many of us, trust remains an elusive concept. We know when it's present and feel when it's absent, but how often do we reflect on our role in building or breaking it?

How *do* we build trust? Is there an art to it? Something we can learn—maybe even master.

Just as a painter may start with a sketch on a clean canvas to guide their painting, building trust begins with a clear framework. For us, that framework is the Reina Dimensions of Trust—or what we call the Three Cs (figure 1).[1]

And, just as an artist uses technique to create height, width, and depth, so too do the Three Dimensions of Trust bring depth

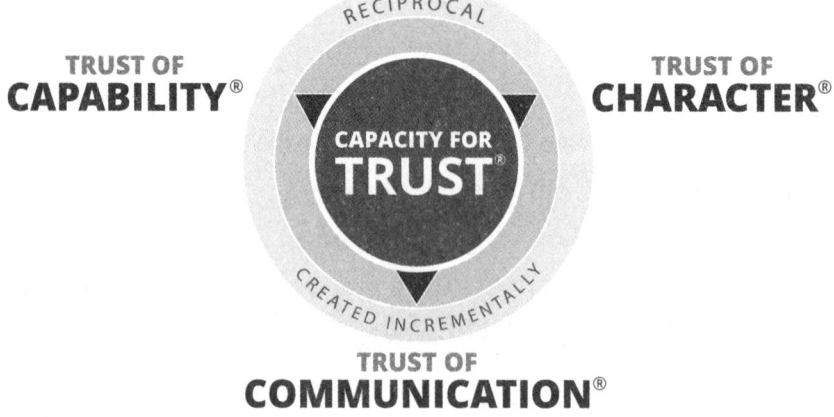

Figure 1. Reina Dimensions of Trust: The Three Cs

and shape to how trust is built. They offer a clear, behavioral road map for growing trust in any relationship. So, let's explore what brings trust to life.

Trust of Character Centers on *Reliability*

Do you do what you say you'll do? Do you keep your promises and honor your commitments? Do you consistently align your actions with your words? Because when you do, you build credibility and foster alignment.

Consider someone who consistently shows up and follows through on commitments—someone you and others can count on to contribute to the success of the team. People know they can depend on this person to deliver results, and that dependability fosters a sense of reliability, confidence, and capability.

Now imagine the opposite: a peer who frequently breaks promises, skipping scheduled meetings without notice and leaving their teammates uncertain and guessing. Over time this inconsistency chips away at trust. You and others become hesitant to engage, everyone begins to pull back, and collaboration breaks down. This is the invisible energy of trust at work—a force that when present, expands, producing results and connection, but when absent, contracts, holding back even the best efforts.

Take Kyle: brilliant but unpredictable. One week he delivered standout work; the next, he missed key meetings and deadlines. Over time, his team lost confidence, collaboration stalled, and his contributions held less weight.

Contrast that with a team that meets weekly, follows through on commitments, and trusts each other to show up. Their consistency creates clarity, alignment, and momentum.

Ideas flow unrestricted, decisions move faster, and results exceed expectations.

What quickly becomes apparent is that when *Trust of Character* is present, people work with shared purpose, understand their roles, and stay committed to each other's success. That level of trust then becomes the engine of performance.

Key behaviors include consistency in managing expectations to meet needs; establishing boundaries; aligning words with actions; keeping agreements; supporting others' success while strengthening your own.

Trust of Communication Centers on *Honesty and Transparency*

Are you willing to speak the truth, even when it's uncomfortable? Do you listen deeply and engage in honest, meaningful dialogue? Do people feel safe bringing sensitive or tough topics to you?

Clear communication is the gateway to open, honest dialogue. It fosters understanding and creates a space where people feel safe sharing ideas, concerns, and vulnerabilities. *Trust of Communication* helps clear the air and reduces uncertainty by encouraging direct, effective conversations. It replaces gossip, rumor, and second-guessing with direct, respectful dialogue. In this environment, no one is left wondering where they stand because everything is out in the open and everyone's on the same page.

When Sarah's team missed a critical deadline, she led with accountability. Instead of blaming, she created a safe space to openly debrief, owned her part, and encouraged others to do the same. Her transparency strengthened trust, deepened collaboration, and reinforced confidence in her leadership.

Trust of Communication establishes the flow of information, deepens connection through truth telling, and supports people to grow by making space for constructive feedback.

Key behaviors include consistency in sharing information transparently; providing what others need; fostering relationships through honest and straightforward communication; admitting mistakes and embracing their lessons; creating a safe space for growth; listening deeply to hear the truth and speaking with positive intention; offering constructive feedback that supports innovation, development, and the best in others.

Trust of Capability Centers on *Acknowledging Skills and Abilities*

Do you empower your peers by involving them in decisions, and acknowledge their efforts and the difference they make? Do you show you believe in their abilities while also supporting them to grow, reach their aspirations, and succeed? Are you contributing to an environment where collaboration and learning can thrive?

Though many doubted Calvin, his teammate Susan saw his potential and offered support. With her encouragement and coaching, he exceeded expectations—delivering early and gaining confidence in himself, thanks to someone who believed in him before he did.

Trust of Capability means believing in *potential*—both your own and others'. While leadership can provide training, development, and resources, it's the consistent everyday encouragement between peers—and each person's dedication to learning—that truly fuels confidence, fosters development, and empowers the whole team to succeed.

Key behaviors include consistency in acknowledging skills and contributions; seeking input; involving others' points of view; encouraging growth; building confidence in your abilities; recognizing your limitations; empowering others to take ownership.

In looking at the key behaviors of the Three Cs, you may have noticed one recurring word: *consistency.* The Three Cs remind us that we can never take trust for granted. Trust must be actively maintained through intentional choices and steady actions. That's why trust is not a one-time achievement, but rather an ongoing commitment to your relationships. Through practicing these behaviors consistently, you create patterns of trustworthiness that strengthen relationships over time. (We explore the concepts of the Three Cs in chapters 2, 3, and 4.)

In a world that is always shifting, even the best intentions get derailed. When our behavior starts to drift, trust can slip. And just like that, we find ourselves in the thick of real trust building challenges.

The Challenges of Trust Building

Trust is inherently vulnerable.

Trust building isn't always easy. It asks a lot from us. It means taking risks, making leaps of faith, believing in others, and being open to the chance that we might get hurt. Let's be real: at some point, your life experience has taught you that trust can and will be broken. Sometimes, it's small things, like a missed deadline, a forgotten promise. Other times, it cuts much deeper, leaving behind scars, lingering doubt, and pain that can remain for a long time.

When trust becomes fragile and begins to crack, it is most often because the Three Cs of Trust aren't being practiced consistently. In that vulnerable space, betrayal can quietly take root and begin to spread.

Consider this: according to our research, 90 percent of the behaviors that break trust are small, subtle, and unintentional—the kind of things that often go unnoticed in the moment.[2]

Trust rarely breaks all at once; rather, it breaks through everyday missteps we all experience or make ourselves: not following through, withholding small pieces of information, making excuses, or forgetting to include someone in a meeting.

In and of themselves, minor infractions of trust may seem innocent. We are inclined to extend grace, give a second chance, offer the benefit of the doubt—yet it's the accumulation of these small, unintentional breaches that results in betrayal.

When trust is breached, relationships suffer a loss. It doesn't just hurt in the present; it steals from the future too—from what the relationships could have been or what opportunities have been lost. The most common reaction is to pull away. People tend to distance themselves from the people who let them down, and the one left behind ends up sitting alone in a swirl of self-doubt, questioning themselves and others.

- *Is this the right place for me?*

- *Am I even good enough?*

- *Do I truly belong here?*

- *Do I have what it takes?*

As doubt creeps in, confidence fades, and forgiveness begins to feel like an uphill climb.

The truth is trust isn't something we build once and then it's done. It gets built, it gets broken, and it gets tested, *repeatedly,* in every relationship. We've all been there, yet this is where trust building provides a new choice: to fixate and brood on the breach or work through the feelings of hurt, disappointment, bitterness, and resentment.

What really counts is recognizing these patterns; discovering how to respond to those tough moments with courageous fortitude, compassionate grace, and a deepened sense of commitment to relationships; and learning to trust again.

The Seven Steps for Healing (figure 2) offer a thoughtful, compassionate path to move through the pain of betrayal and broken trust.[3] They guide you to find the courage to face what happened, honor what you are feeling, and begin to uncover the lessons hidden inside the hurt. With this clarity born out of honest reflection, you can take conscious responsibility for your own healing while also working toward rebuilding meaningful relationships—because if you don't deal with the disconnection, the distance only grows, and the pain of disconnection becomes too great to heal.

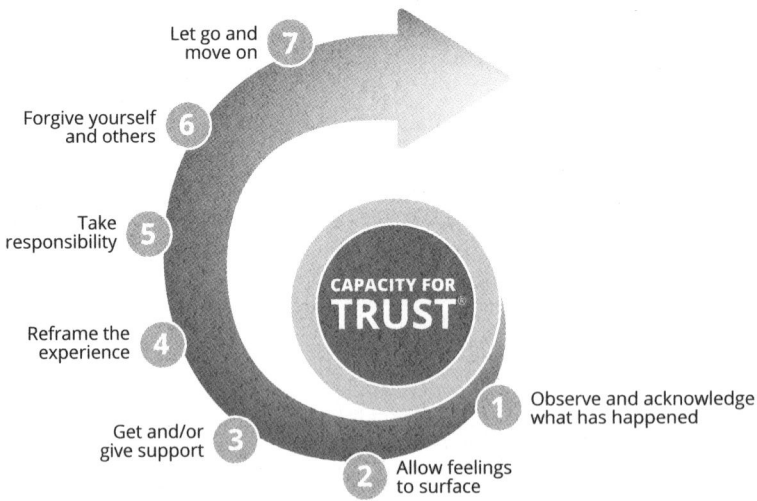

Figure 2. Seven Steps for Healing

Rebuilding trust doesn't happen overnight. It takes introspection, thoughtful reflection, and a conscious choice to act with courage and compassion. While it's challenging, the rewards are profound—we know this firsthand from our research and our personal and professional experience.

Back in 2000, a year after the first edition of *Trust and Betrayal in the Workplace* was published, we found ourselves tested in a deeply personal way.

One of those commitments involved a high-stakes client project. Dennis was diagnosed with renal carcinoma and was convalescing after having a kidney removed. So, Michelle reached out to a trusted colleague for help, and the colleague assured her the work would be delivered on time. But the deadline came and went—with no update, no delivery, and no explanation. Michelle was left scrambling. Hurt and stressed, she did what she could: found a solution quickly, owned the mistake with the client, and stayed honest and accountable throughout.

Later, she learned her colleague had been dealing with her daughter's overdose and was too overwhelmed and ashamed to explain. Understanding the pain all too well, Michelle chose compassion over blame. She forgave her colleague, not just to ease the tension, but to open a door for healing.

Rebuilding trust is never easy—but the rewards can be worth it when we commit to doing the inner work. It calls for real courage to dig deep and acknowledge what happened; compassion to consider what might have been going on beneath the surface, to extend the benefit of the doubt, to forgive our human imperfection; and a willingness to take responsibility—even when you've been hurt. Chapter 5 gives you greater insight into what causes trust to break down, and chapter 6 guides you through the Seven

Steps, a path designed to offer you a process and practice tools for each step of the way.

The beauty of rebuilding trust is that it creates a stronger foundation than before. It deepens connection, builds resilience, and sparks real, lasting growth. And it all starts with one powerful decision: *the choice to trust again.*

This doesn't mean you won't forget the hurt or pretend it didn't happen. It means reaching a place—often unexpectedly—where gratitude begins to take root. Not gratitude for the breach of trust, but for what came out of it: the lessons, the insights, the strength you discovered in yourself, and the wisdom you gained—wisdom you can offer to others as a gift from your own healing.

And here's the beautiful part: when you give from that space, the law of reciprocity kicks in. What you offer—trust, grace, truth—has a way of coming back to you, even stronger.

That's why *the art of trust building* requires courageously embracing vulnerability as a strength to be leveraged in renewing trust in yourself—and your willingness to trust others—with compassion as your North Star.

The Art of Trust Building as an Unfolding Journey

We define trust building as a transformative practice involving the intentional process of cultivating, strengthening, and sustaining trust through deliberate actions, authentic communication, and shared vulnerability.

When you commit to this journey (figure 3), it becomes a deep source of strength. It asks you to look within, not through a checklist of traits, but with honest reflection. This is not just about

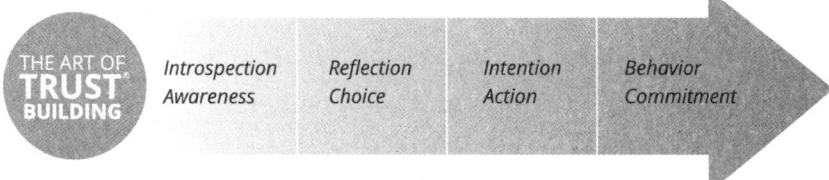

Figure 3. The Art of Trust Building

improvement—it's a soulful journey of introspection that lays the groundwork for transforming lives, teams, and organizations.

The art of trust building begins with a willingness to look inward. It's through honest introspection that you raise your self-awareness and begin to see the deeper patterns shaping how you show up in the world. This inner work becomes the gateway to meaningful growth—not just within yourself, but in every relationship you touch.

As you reflect, you begin to see more clearly. You gain the wisdom to choose how you want to engage—with empathy, kindness, and a heart-centered presence. Rather than reacting out of habit or fear, you shift toward becoming more intentional about your words, your actions, and your impact. In this shift, something deeper begins to take root: conviction.

Conviction in relationships is the quiet strength that fuels your consistency. It's the inner belief that trust is worth building—even when it's hard, even when it's slow. It's a commitment to show up fully, to communicate honestly, and to stand in alignment with your values. When trust building is grounded in conviction, it becomes more than a choice—it becomes a way of honoring both yourself and the people you care about.

Trust building isn't about perfection—it's about being present. It's about knowing you're a part of something larger than yourself and letting that awareness guide how you show up. With conviction and clarity, you act with positive intentions in how you connect with, support, and stand beside others.

At its core, trust building is a daily practice—it's a way of living. Rooted in your values, reflected in your choices, and sustained by your commitment to grow, trust becomes the rhythm of how you live and lead. Moment by moment, conversation by conversation, you craft something meaningful.

This is where transformation occurs. When trust building is grounded by conviction, it becomes more than a personal practice—it becomes a cultural force. It shapes the way we work, live, and lead together. Transformation takes root here.

And with that transformation often comes a deep sense of gratitude—gratitude for the growth, for the courage it takes to show up fully, and for the people who choose to meet us in that space. Gratitude inspires us to honor the journey and embrace the art of trust building not as a task, but as a way of being. It reminds us that trust is not just built—it's cherished.

And with that transformation, we build the foundation for lasting change. That is the art of trust building.

Whether you're a member of a team, leading a unit, building a business, or nurturing personal connections, trust is the invisible thread that fortifies the fabric of meaningful human interaction. The trust building behaviors shared throughout this book are here to guide you in creating relationships—at work and in life—that are rooted in mutual respect, honesty, and care.

So, *where* will you begin? Better yet, *when*?

Trust building is a journey—and every meaningful journey begins with a first step. To create the trust you deserve, you need clarity, intention, and the right tools to guide you.

Before you turn the page, take a moment to complete the Reina Individual Trust Scale Assessment. This self-assessment will offer a clear, honest snapshot of how trust is currently showing up in your life—within yourself and in how you engage with others.

The insights you gain will serve as a powerful foundation for the work ahead. With this book as your guide, you'll be equipped to build trust more intentionally, navigate challenges with greater confidence, and foster deeper, more meaningful connection across every part of your life.

Start here.

Take the assessment.

Your trust building journey begins now.

reinatrustbuilding.com/ITS-book

CHAPTER ONE

The Starting Line

Trust Begins with You

If you trust yourself, you will know how to live.
JOHANN WOLFGANG VON GOETHE

Trust building is more than an ideological concept or aspirational idea to strive for: it's an invisible energy field that connects you to yourself and others, as well as the unlimited possibilities that exist at these intersections.

Take, for example, Emma.

Emma had spent most of her life second-guessing herself. Even small decisions stirred up anxiety: What if I get it wrong? What if I'm not enough?

So, when she was asked to lead a major community project—a fundraising event to save the neighborhood library—her immediate reaction was to decline. It felt too big, too public, too far outside her comfort zone.

But with gentle encouragement from her mentor, who reminded her she already had what she needed, Emma decided to go for it. And yet the night before the first meeting, her old doubts once again crept in: I'm not a leader.

I'm going to mess this up. Despite the nervousness and
uncertainty, she showed up.

The meeting wasn't flawless. She stumbled over words and
forgot a few key points, but despite all of this, something unexpected unfolded: people responded. They listened, nodded,
and offered their support. Encouraged, Emma continued. Each
step forward helped quiet her inner critic. What she eventually
realized is that self-trust isn't about knowing everything—it's
about believing you can figure things out along the way.

On the day of the event, the library buzzed with energy.
The result was that they exceeded their fundraising goal.
Emma, standing tall in the middle of it all, felt something
she hadn't in a long time—pride. Not because she had done
everything perfectly, but because she had trusted herself
enough to begin.

Whether it's with family, friends, or coworkers, at the core of
building lasting trust is self-awareness. Through self-awareness,
you form a deeper connection to yourself. When you're connected
to yourself, you are truly in tune with how you see yourself, how
you relate to others, and how you handle life's uncertainties. You
lay the groundwork for meaningful, lasting relationships. All of
this is to say—**trust begins with you**. This includes how you perceive yourself, relate to others, and navigate the uncertainties of
your life.

Throughout this chapter, we will be exploring

- **Where your trust begins**

- **Trusting yourself**

- **Trusting others**

It's undeniable that trusting in yourself is a deeply personal journey shaped by your life experiences. From the moment you are born, your Capacity for Trust influences every part of your life—family, friends, social groups, teams, romantic relationships, work communities, faith—and how you see the world.

Developing and evolving trust is rooted in your self-awareness, which includes your attitude, outlook, and beliefs that shape how you choose to trust and navigate life's challenges and triumphs.

When you learn to see trust as your inner compass, you unlock deeper connection with yourself and with others. You move through life with greater courage, compassion, and commitment to relationships.

Where Your Trust Begins

Your Capacity for Trust (figure 4) begins the moment you enter the world and is influenced by the care and consistency you receive from your earliest relationships.[1] Some people are fortunate to grow up in nurturing environments filled with safety,

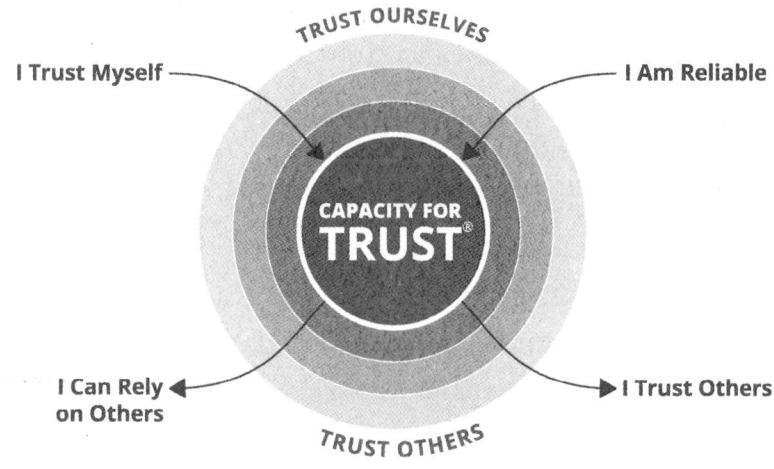

Figure 4. Capacity for Trust

support, and reliability. Others have faced inconsistent or more challenging beginnings, leading to a reserved, protective, and cautious approach to trust. These early experiences lay the foundation for how you trust *yourself* and others.

For those who grew up in a mix of calm and chaos, trust— like energy—tends to ebb and flow, expand and contract. It wasn't the uncertainty itself that shaped your capacity to trust but how your caregivers handled it. When uncertainty was met with reassurance and stability, trust had space to grow. But if it was met with inconsistency, trust may have felt fragile. Even if those early experiences led to a more cautious or guarded approach, your capacity to trust is not fixed. Through greater self-awareness and intentional choices in how you build trust— with yourself and with others—your capacity to trust can evolve and deepen over time.

Let's take a moment to explore what we mean by your Capacity for Trust. **Capacity for Trust is your willingness and readiness to trust yourself and others.** This capacity expands and contracts throughout your life based on your unfolding experiences. It influences your perceptions and beliefs about *yourself and others*, ultimately influencing how you bring yourself to relationships. For instance, if you see yourself as trustworthy, you project that trustworthiness outward. Conversely, if you struggle to trust yourself, that struggle can hinder your ability to connect with others and feel secure in uncertain situations.

At its core, trust is deeply tied to self-awareness. It asks you to be introspective and reflective about how you think, feel, and choose to behave. It requires thoughtful choices in how you behave and how you stay true to yourself. **Trust building isn't just a value or belief—it's a *practice* demonstrated through actions.** The more aware you become about what's going on inside you, the stronger your connections become—with your-self, with others, and with your sense of purpose.

Trusting Yourself: The Starting Point

Trusting yourself is fundamental to who you are and how you relate to the world. When you trust yourself, you feel centered, confident, and capable of fulfilling expectations. This inner trust impacts your self-esteem and relationships. People who trust themselves are more likely to be trusted by others. However, trusting yourself isn't always easy, especially when you're dealing with doubt, setbacks, or change. This begets the question: *Why is it that some of us struggle to trust ourselves?*

While many things in the external world feel uncertain, the one thing we all share is the presence of our inner voice, which is always speaking to us. For many, the struggle with self-trust begins here—because that inner voice often shows up as self-doubt or harsh criticism. This is what we all know as the "the inner critic," that part that quietly questions:

- *Can I really do this?*

- *Am I good enough?*

- *Am I capable of rising to new challenges?*

- *Will I say and do the right things in my relationships?*

We've all wrestled with these kinds of doubts, especially during uncertainty or when the stakes are high. Without a strong sense of self-trust, these doubts can hold us back, paralyze us, and cause us to shy away from challenges or avoid seeking help. Negative thoughts, *fueled by the experiences of past failures or criticism*, become ingrained as self-talk, undermining our confidence and trust in our abilities.

So, how do you strengthen your self-trust?

Building self-trust begins by paying attention to your thoughts—both the positive ones that lift you up and the ones that hold you back. When negative thoughts arise, pause and question them.

Ask yourself, *Is this true?* Step back and consider the bigger picture. Perhaps these thoughts are rooted in past fears, not in current truths. Be aware of how past experiences may distort or exaggerate the present truth.

Self-trust is the glue that holds you together in difficult times and the spark that fuels meaningful growth. It gives you the confidence to face challenges, grounded in the belief that you have what it takes to navigate the unknown. With self-trust, you're more willing to take risks, try new things, and approach obstacles with courage and resilience. It becomes the foundation that allows you to move forward—boldly and with purpose—no matter what lies ahead.

Trusting Others

After years of unmet expectations and disappointment by others in her corporate career, Sophie had learned to be cautious with trust. Her instinct was to stay in control—to protect outcomes by managing every detail herself. So, when she was tasked with leading a high-stakes client presentation with a new team, every part of her told her to take charge and "do it herself."

But this time, she chose differently. She chose to trust.

Rather than micromanage, Sophie took a more intentional approach. She assessed each person's strengths, set clear expectations, and stayed actively engaged—without controlling every move. When a teammate hit a rough patch, she didn't step in to take over. She offered support, not judgment.

That decision changed everything. The team delivered a flawless presentation and landed a major deal.

More importantly, Sophie discovered that trust isn't unquestioning belief or wishful thinking—it's a bold choice rooted in clarity, accountability, and empowerment. Trust doesn't mean letting go of standards or outcomes. It means creating the space for others to rise—and thrive—especially when it matters most.

The Art of Trust Building

When you expand your Capacity for Trust, you improve your relationships and open doors for greater success. Remember: trust is reciprocal—the more you extend trust, the more you receive it in return.

These four essential questions are designed to help you reflect on your readiness and willingness to trust. Our intention is to help you become more aware of the signs and indicators that tell you that you are reluctant to trust. We equip you with action steps to choose from to guide your growth and expand your capacity to trust. Let's explore each question.

1. How Realistic Are You?

Have you ever felt stuck—like doing nothing seemed safer than taking a chance?

If so, you might be experiencing *contracted realism*. It's a mindset where fear and doubt shrink your view of what's possible, making you focus more on what could go wrong than what could go right. The first step toward breaking free from that mindset is self-awareness. Can you recognize any of these three patterns showing up in your life right now?

You focus on limitations more than possibilities. Instead of imagining what could go right, your mind goes straight to what might go wrong. When new opportunities show up, you hesitate—waiting for absolute certainty before making a move, even when the potential payoff is meaningful.

You set unrealistic or rigid expectations. You expect perfection from yourself or others, leaving little room for missteps. When things don't go as planned, it throws you off. Trust becomes tied to flawless execution instead of the ability to adapt when life takes a different turn.

You resist adjusting your assumptions. You lean heavily on past experiences as evidence things won't change. If something didn't work before, you assume it still won't work. You might make quick judgments about people or situations and brush off new perspectives—because it feels safer to stick with what you already know and believe.

Do any of these signs feel familiar? If yes, you're not alone. Take a moment to extend compassion to yourself. It's natural to feel unsure or vulnerable in unfamiliar situations. The encouraging part is that you have a choice.

Let's explore ways you can exercise that choice to expand your capacity for trust and balance realism.

Shift from *What if it fails?* to *What if it works?* When you catch yourself focusing on what could go wrong, pause and ask: *What's the best that could happen?* Reflect on moments from your past when things worked out—even when the outcome was uncertain. Remind yourself that growth often happens outside your comfort zone and, sometimes, trusting the unknown is exactly what moves you forward.

Redefine success as progress, not perfection. Remember, mistakes aren't failures—they're part of the learning process. Set goals that are both flexible and realistic, giving yourself room to adapt as you grow. Along the way, celebrate small wins; they help build trust not only in your own abilities but in others' as well.

Reframe assumptions with a fresh perspective. When doubt creeps in, ask yourself: *Is this really the same situation, or could it turn out differently this time?* Give people and circumstances the space to surprise you—in a good way. Stay curious, because a fresh perspective can often reveal new possibilities you hadn't seen before.

Expanding your realism doesn't mean abandoning caution or ignoring risks—it means recognizing potential and possibility alongside risks. It's about staying open, adjusting your expectations, and being willing to grow. And it all starts with simply noticing patterns.

2. Do You Need to "See It to Believe It"?

"Seeing it to believe it" reflects how you respond to others' promises or decisions. Do you trust them? Or do you need concrete proof first?

If you can take people at their word, you're likely comfortable with ambiguity and open to collaboration. But if you consistently need evidence before moving forward, you may be operating from a contracted trust mindset—driven more by control than connection. This can create roadblocks to delegation, innovation, and progress.

The key is to ask: *Is my need for proof protecting me—or keeping me stuck?* Recognizing this pattern is the first step toward expanding your Capacity for Trust by balancing discernment with openness. Here are three simple steps to help you address this pattern.

Start small. Trust doesn't have to begin with big leaps. Begin with small, meaningful gestures—delegate a task, take someone at their word, or offer the benefit of the doubt. These simple acts lay the groundwork for your trust to grow and build confidence over time.

Rethink uncertainty. Trust isn't naive without discernment —it's about creating space for people to show you who they are. When doubt creeps in, pause and ask: *Have they shown up before? Am I responding to the moment or past fear?*

Find the middle ground. Wanting proof is human—but trust also needs openness. Instead of waiting for every detail to line up, act when you have enough to move forward.

Trust often grows once you take that first step. It's natural to want certainty—but trust requires openness and faith. Instead of waiting for perfect clarity, move when you have enough to take a step. Often, trust deepens once you're in motion.

3. Do You Generalize Based on Past Experiences?

Let's be honest—**we've all been burned before.** And those experiences shape how willing we are to trust again. But here's the question: *Are you giving each person a fair shot? Or are old disappointments quietly shaping how you approach new relationships?*

It's easy to let one negative experience cast a long shadow. A friend's betrayal might make you pull back emotionally. A colleague's failure could lead you to think no one at work can be counted on. Before you know it, you're guarding yourself—not just from that one person, but from everyone.

When your **trust is contracted**, you may start expecting people to let you down. You might judge quickly, assume the worst, or hold others to standards they didn't agree to—just because someone in the past hurt you. The result? Missed opportunities, strained connections, and unnecessary distance. Sometimes without realizing it, you start to judge others too quickly, expecting them to let you down simply because someone else did. You might assume they should think or act the way you do, which can lead to unrealistic expectations. When that happens, it's easy to pull away from people who are different from you and miss out on meaningful connections or creative solutions.

In these moments, trust isn't based on what's happening now but on past hurt—and that can make it much harder to build the kinds of relationships that lead to real growth, collaboration, and belonging. When you find yourself sliding into this space, here are a few ways to move beyond generalizations that limit trust so you can approach others with more openness and clarity:

Pause assumptions. When you catch yourself judging someone based on a past hurt, ask: *Is this really the same situation—or am I replaying an old story?* Give people a chance to show who they are now, not who they used to be—or who someone else was.

Loosen expectations. People may act differently than you would. That doesn't make them untrustworthy—just different. Instead of expecting others to match your style, try asking: *What can I learn from the way they show up?*

Expand your comfort zone. Try connecting with people who think, look, or live differently than you do. Start small. Stay curious. Listen with openness. When something feels unfamiliar, ask: *What might this new perspective teach me?*

By questioning assumptions and staying open to diverse perspectives, you make room for deeper trust to grow. This not only strengthens your relationships but also invites new opportunities, fresh insights, and meaningful connections you might not have expected.

4. How Comfortable Are You Operating in the Gray?

Life doesn't always fit into tidy boxes of right or wrong, good or bad, black or white. An expanded Capacity for Trust helps you to navigate the gray areas—those moments filled with uncertainty, nuance, and complexity. It allows you to stay open and to embrace ambiguity by considering multiple perspectives and responding to complexity with openness and adaptability. In this space, you can appreciate the strengths and vulnerabilities of others, leading to stronger connections and wiser decisions—even when the path forward isn't entirely clear.

But when trust is contracted, you may fall into black-and-white thinking. You might rush to judgment or resist different viewpoints or see challenges as threats instead of growth opportunities. That kind of rigidity narrows your view and can lead to premature conclusions and strained relationships.

To shift out of this rigid, all-or-nothing mindset, you can practice the art of trust building—simple, intentional steps that help you stay open, grounded, and connected even when things feel uncertain.

Here's how to begin:

Choose curiosity over certainty. When things feel unclear, resist the urge to label or judge. Stay open. Ask questions, explore different views, and allow new possibilities to emerge.

Build the courage to sit with discomfort. Trusting in the "gray" means accepting that not everything has a quick or tidy answer. When you feel the need to control or react, pause. Breathe. Growth often happens in the unknown—growth often happens in the space of uncertainty.

Begin with acts of trust. Start small—invite someone's input, try on a new perspective, or take a step forward with just enough information. These simple acts help you strengthen your self-trust and ease your way through ambiguity.

When you trust in yourself, you create the capacity to trust others. Through reflection and intentional action, you build relationships grounded in connection, collaboration, and mutual understanding. Trusting wisely means learning from the past *without living in it*. Yes, people have let you down—but people also change. So do you. And trust deserves the chance to grow with you.

In the next three chapters, you will be exploring the Three Dimensions of Trust that equip you with the behaviors to practice trust building as a way of life. Because at the heart of it all—*trust building begins with you*.

CHAPTER TWO

Trust of Character

*Building the Foundation for
Relationships and Success*

> *The greatest discovery of any generation is that a human
> being can alter their life by altering their attitude.*
> JAMES ALLEN

At the heart of every lasting relationship, personal or professional, is Trust of Character—the anchor that grounds connection and the foundation upon which meaningful relationships and strong teams are built. Without it, relationships drift, leaving people searching for clarity, direction, and purpose.

Trust of Character isn't passive.[1] It's earned through deliberate, consistent action. More than just good intentions or kind words, it's about honoring commitments, being reliable, and showing up with integrity—especially in times of uncertainty, vulnerability, or change. When people trust your character, you become a steady, grounding force that fosters alignment, resilience, and forward momentum.

At its core, Trust of Character is the alignment between what you say and what you do. It's integrity made visible, as well as how others experience your values in action. Moving forward, as you reflect on how others perceive your character, consider: *Do my actions match my intentions? Am I someone others can count on—no matter the circumstances?*

Through our years of research, we have found Trust of Character (figure 5) is established through six key behaviors:

- Manage expectations.

- Establish boundaries.

- Delegate appropriately.

- Encourage mutually serving intentions.

- Keep agreements.

- Be consistent.

When you consistently practice these behaviors, trust becomes visible and actionable. You create an environment where reliability, mutual respect, and credibility naturally grow—transforming trust building from a passive concept into a lived experience.

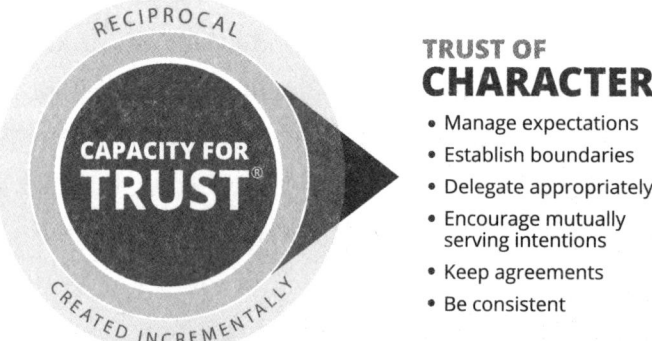

Figure 5. Trust of Character

Trust of Character isn't just about avoiding missteps—it's about cultivating a culture of dependability and connection. It's the foundation that allows people to feel safe, contribute fully, and thrive. When your actions consistently reflect integrity, people see who you truly are, and they're drawn to work with you, not just because of what you do, but because of how you show up in the world.

Manage Expectations

From the moment you wake up, your days are shaped by expectations you place on yourself and others. These often-unspoken agreements guide your actions, influence your communication, and shape your relationships. At their core, expectations reflect underlying needs, and when those needs are met, trust grows, and relationships strengthen.

When expectations are not met, misalignment, frustration, and breakdowns in trust often follow.

In today's fast-moving, tech-driven, and often virtual work environments, expectations frequently shift, making alignment a moving target. Even well-intentioned teams can falter when expectations aren't clear, leading to missed deadlines, stalled projects, and growing frustration.

Expectations serve as a blueprint for collaboration, guiding actions, building momentum, and enabling success. This is why clear expectations matter—especially during uncertainty, amid periods of change, or when working across different cultures. Clear expectations help everyone stay aligned in a shared purpose, giving individuals the clarity and confidence they need to do their best work.

For a moment, think back to a time when expectations weren't clear—when you didn't know what was expected until it was too late, or when someone let you down without realizing it. These moments highlight how unspoken expectations can quietly erode trust.

Often occurring in times of transition, we automatically assume others know what we need, or we believe we understand their needs, without clearly stating them. Such a lack of clarity creates tension, weakens trust, and disrupts collaboration.

> *As an example, Tom, a software developer, was asked to create a "user-friendly and secure" app feature. Interpreting the request on his own, he spent weeks building a complex interface with advanced security. But when he presented it, his manager was disappointed—what was needed was a simple, intuitive design with basic security. Tom's well-intentioned effort missed the mark due to a lack of clarity and shared understanding.*

This misalignment of expectations led to wasted effort and delayed timelines. The lesson? *Vague instructions and unclarified expectations often result in inefficiency.*

The Art of Managing Expectations

Expectations are the silent architects of interaction.

The first step to managing expectations is simple but powerful: tune in to your needs and clearly communicate them. When expectations are shared, people can align, support each other, and do their best work.

In new or uncertain situations, assumptions often fill in the gaps. While they can be helpful, the key is recognizing them and checking in with others to avoid misunderstandings. Assumptions aren't the problem—failing to test them is.

Clear communication is not about rigidity; it's about *alignment*. When everyone understands the goals and how to achieve them, you create a foundation for collaboration and mutual respect. As such, trust is a two-way street built on reciprocity and mutual understanding. When you clearly communicate your expectations, you offer others the clarity they need to succeed. Equally important to defining your own expectations is understanding what others need from you.

Trust is inherently reciprocal—a two-way street grounded in mutual understanding and shared responsibility. When you clearly communicate your expectations, you offer the clarity others need to thrive. Just as vital is your attentiveness to what others expect from you, creating a dynamic exchange of clarity and support.

People want to deliver and support one another, but that only happens when we take the time to ask and listen. Whether you're leading a team or collaborating with a colleague, the right questions can open the door to clarity and connection. The following questions foster transparency, reduce friction, and create shared ownership:

- *What kind of tools or support would help you feel more confident in your work right now and be most helpful to you?*

- *Are there any challenges or obstacles you foresee that we should plan for together?*

- *What does success look like for both of us?*

A hallmark of managing expectations well is making the implicit explicit—clearly defining what success looks like, what's needed to achieve it, and what kind of support is required. These conversations build trust, strengthen collaboration, and align intention with outcomes—even amid uncertainty.

During times of change or stress, unspoken expectations can create even greater strain. Without clear communication, assumptions take over—and that's when confusion and misalignment surface.

> *Take Emma and Jordan. They thought they were aligned on a client presentation—Emma would handle strategy, Jordan the data. But when a last-minute request came in to include detailed metrics, neither clarified who would respond. Each assumed the other would handle it, and the next morning, that oversight led to a scramble and unnecessary stress. A simple check-in—"How should we handle this change?"—could have prevented the issue.*

The takeaway? Clear communication is essential—not just at the start of a project, but especially when plans shift. In moments of uncertainty, don't rely on assumptions. Instead, take the time to make the implicit explicit.

When circumstances change, expectations often need to shift too. Rather than risk misalignment, be proactive. Acknowledge the change and its impact, invite support, and work together to create realistic alternatives—whether it's adjusting timelines, redistributing responsibilities, or redefining priorities. This keeps momentum moving forward.

Renegotiation isn't about making excuses; it's about taking ownership with honesty and respect. When you address changes directly, you show reliability and you reinforce trust—even when things are uncertain.

The bottom line? Like all facets of trust, managing expectations begins with you.

Mastering the Art of Managing Expectations

Managing expectations takes intention, courage, and a willingness to engage in honest dialogue—especially when the stakes are high. Done well, it builds clarity, strengthens connection, and deepens trust. These key steps will help you practice this path with confidence:

Start with introspection. Before setting expectations, take a moment to get clear on what you truly need—from yourself and from others. Are your expectations realistic, specific, and free of assumptions? Self-awareness is the first act of courage.

Speak up early and compassionately. Don't assume others know what you need—speak up, ask questions, and check for understanding as situations evolve. Compassion and clarity work together.

Make sure you're on the same page. Mutual understanding is everything. Confirm what's been agreed, clarify roles, and make sure everyone is aligned. Clarity prevents confusion before it starts.

Stay open and flexible. Life shifts, and so do people's needs. Be willing to adjust; listen with empathy; seek and offer support as things evolve. Flexibility isn't weakness—it's wisdom in action.

Reflect and realign together. Check in regularly. Ask, *Is this still working for both of us?* Use these moments to reflect, reset, and realign about what matters now. Ongoing alignment keeps expectations healthy and human.

Follow through with heart. Trust grows when you do what you say you'll do. Stay consistent. And, when things shift, communicate honestly and take ownership. Integrity in action builds lasting trust.

Managing expectations is a courageous and intentional act that begins with self-awareness and unfolds through honest, compassionate dialogue. It requires clarity about your own needs, the willingness to communicate openly, and a commitment to mutual understanding. By staying flexible, checking in regularly, and following through with integrity, you not only prevent confusion but also cultivate trust, strengthen relationships, and create space for deeper connection.

Establish Boundaries

Boundaries are often misunderstood. Boundaries aren't walls that separate us—they're bridges that help us stay connected in healthy, sustainable ways, especially during change. Clear boundaries define how we work, communicate, and collaborate. They eliminate guesswork, prevent misunderstandings, and foster mutual respect and trust within teams and organizations.

The Art of Establishing Boundaries

Boundaries show up in many ways—managing time, respecting privacy and space, maintaining professionalism, and understanding what's appropriate to ask, say, or expect. When well defined, they guide workflow and help people understand their roles and responsibilities and how they fit into the bigger picture.

But know that boundaries don't need to be rigid. Permeable boundaries—those that are clear but flexible—create agility and allow teams to adapt, share information freely, and uncover opportunities for innovation and collaboration. When grounded in shared purpose and clarity, these flexible boundaries support real connection and forward momentum.

However, when boundaries are vague or inconsistent, they create confusion. Team members may second-guess their roles, hesitate to act, or fear stepping on toes—ultimately stifling initiative, creativity, and collaboration.

Mastering the Art of Establishing Boundaries

Setting boundaries within a team isn't just a trust building practice—it's an ongoing practice toward mastery. It begins by clearly defining the team's purpose, roles, and responsibilities. A strong starting point is to align around core questions:

- *What problems are we here to solve?*

- *Who do we serve—internally or externally?*

- *What unique value do we bring?*

Start by reflecting on the impact your team aspires to have. This creates a sense of connection to a shared purpose and strengthens commitment to the collective mission.

Next, help your team define the team's responsibilities—projects, deliverables, and key tasks. Clarify the value you contribute to the broader organization. Then support them to consider the needs of stakeholders, identify any overlaps or gaps, and use this clarity to turn potential confusion into effective collaboration.

When team members actively participate in shaping these boundaries, a sense of shared ownership emerges. This fosters trust, promotes mutual accountability, and supports a healthier,

more productive culture. Like any meaningful art, boundary setting requires consistent attention, honest communication, and
care over time.

Delegate Appropriately

> *When Nina was asked to lead a new client proposal, she*
> *was eager to prove herself. But as she worked, her manager,*
> *Mark, micromanaged every step—questioning her choices,*
> *changing her work, and overriding her decisions. What*
> *should have been an empowering opportunity left Nina*
> *frustrated and unsure of herself. The message? Mark didn't*
> *trust her—and over time, she stopped trusting herself.*

Delegation is meant to be an act of empowerment—a signal
of trust that fuels growth, strengthens relationships, and prepares
people for future success. But when it's clouded by micromanagement, like in Mark's case, it sends a conflicting message: *I trust*
you . . . but not really. The result is stifled growth, diminished
self-confidence, and eroded morale.

Delegation is often misunderstood. It's not about offloading
tasks for convenience—it's about taking responsibility for how
goals are achieved with and through others. Everyone involved
should be clear on that intent.

When done well, delegation communicates belief in someone's abilities. It boosts morale, builds confidence, and opens
doors for skill development and leadership. But when done
poorly—through micromanagement or complete abdication—it
undermines trust and damages relationships. No one wants to
be used as a dumping ground. In short, how you delegate speaks
volumes about the trust you extend.

The Art of Delegating Appropriately

Delegation is often seen as a top-down process—something a manager does by assigning tasks. But delegation also happens between peers, and it doesn't always look formal. Sometimes, it's as simple as asking for help or passing a task to someone whose strengths or interests are a better fit. Whether it comes from a leader or a colleague, true delegation isn't just about handing off work—it's about creating opportunity and empowering others to contribute in meaningful ways.

Effective delegation fosters growth, builds trust, and develops skills. It offers structure by setting clear expectations, offering the right resources, and granting appropriate authority. When done well, delegation empowers others to succeed—and shows your confidence in their abilities.

But there's a critical distinction to be made—delegation is not abdication.

- **Delegation** is intentional and supportive. It includes guidance, mentoring, resources, and communication.

- **Abdication** leaves someone to figure things out alone, without direction or support, often setting them up to fail.

Think about a time when you were given a task without any direction or support. It can leave you feeling overwhelmed, uncertain, and unsure of where to begin. Delegation, on the other hand, offers clarity and support. For example, instead of saying, *You're in charge of this project*, try: *Here's the goal and the timeline—what support or resources do you need?*

This simple shift signals your investment in their success, reinforces accountability, and builds trust.

On the other end of the spectrum lies micromanagement—another common pitfall. While abdication gives too little support, micromanagement imposes too much control. It sends a mixed message: *I trust you . . . but I need to monitor everything you do.* This can stifle creativity, erode confidence, and strain relationships.

If you notice this pattern in yourself, ask: *Where is my need to control coming from?* Often, it traces back to early experiences or learned behaviors—not from the person in front of you.

Ultimately, effective delegation is about letting go of control—not presence. It means trusting others to take ownership while staying available to support. When you delegate with confidence in someone's potential, you do more than get the job done—you empower growth, build confidence, and help others learn to trust themselves.

Delegation done well doesn't just move the work forward—it moves people forward.

Mastering the Art of Delegating Appropriately

When Ava's manager, Daniel, asked her to lead a major product launch, she hesitated—unsure she was ready. But Daniel's belief in her, paired with his offer of support, gave her the confidence to move forward.

As she led the project, Ava discovered her own strengths. Daniel's delegation wasn't just about assigning a task—it was an act of trust that empowered Ava to grow. This is the true power of delegation: it creates space for people to rise.

To master delegation, start by asking yourself: *Am I empowering others or holding them back? Am I providing the right support? Am I creating space for growth?*

Answering these questions honestly helps you refine your approach and unlock the full potential of your team.

Delegation is an art—balancing clarity with flexibility, guidance with autonomy, and trust with accountability. So, the next time you're tempted to do it all yourself, pause—and choose to delegate with intention. When you invest in others' success, you not only reach your goals—you build a culture of trust and shared achievement.

Encourage Mutually Serving Intentions

Every lasting, successful relationship is built on a commitment to mutual success. Trust thrives when you care as deeply about others' goals and well-being as you do your own. You take genuine interest in your peers—not just in what they do, but in who they are and where they are headed.

Although you continue to pursue your own ambitions, your actions aren't self-serving. You operate with others in mind, guided by a spirit of purpose, generosity, and shared support. This is where trust takes root—and where true collaboration begins.

This mindset of mutually serving intentions strengthens connection, builds trust, gives you the courage to step into the unknown and stretch beyond your comfort zone, and frees you to explore new possibilities, knowing others have your back. It transforms relationships, deepens collaboration, and anchors teams in mutual respect.

But let's be honest: practicing this mindset isn't always easy, especially under pressure. When stress is high, it's easy to slip into self-preservation. We go inward. The focus shifts to me—my deadlines, my stress, my need to feel in control. To look good. It's not that you don't care—it's that you are consumed with protecting your own ground. But when self-protection takes the lead, connection takes a back seat.

You become guarded. Without meaning to, you might unintentionally shut others out, overlook their input, or respond with impatience or frustration—leaving people feeling dismissed or even betrayed. You stay focused on protecting yourself instead of staying open to connection. Over time, these patterns chip away at trust and create a culture of defensiveness.

We've all seen the impact of self-serving behavior—when someone assumes credit that isn't theirs, dismisses others' contributions, or consistently steers conversations to serve their own agenda. These patterns erode trust, fracture teamwork, and stifle collaboration.

In contrast, when shared purpose and mutual support drive behavior, everything shifts. People listen more openly, contribute more freely, and face challenges side by side. Trust becomes more than a value—it becomes a living force that fuels creativity, strengthens relationships, and carries the whole team forward, together.

The Art of Encouraging Mutually Serving Intentions

When mutually serving intentions become the norm, their impact reaches far beyond individual tasks. Agendas are transparent, motivations are trusted, and communication becomes more open and inclusive. People stop second-guessing each other and begin working with greater alignment and ease. As individuals feel seen and supported, creativity grows, resilience strengthens, and a powerful sense of shared purpose begins to take root.

Consider Sofia and Raj, leaders of the product and marketing teams. When they noticed ongoing misalignment was stalling collaboration, they created space for open dialogue. Team members shared goals, challenges, and expectations.

Sofia made sure everyone had a voice, while Raj helped the group see differences as strengths. By exploring each person's underlying motivations, the team began to uncover shared interests and align their efforts. What began as friction turned into flow, advancing both individual and collective goals with greater trust and synergy.

But practicing mutually serving intentions is hardest when stress kicks in—moments of ambiguity, pressure, and fear can trigger self-preservation. Ironically, these are the moments when the principle matters most. Holding others' needs in high regard, even when you feel vulnerable, reinforces trust and strengthens relationships.

Losing sight of others' needs can shift you into a self-focused mindset that damages connections.

Often, it's not big betrayals but small, subtle, everyday actions that do the most damage—a dismissive tone, a missed opportunity to acknowledge someone's input, or leaving someone out of a decision. These seemingly small moments can send a powerful message: you don't matter here. Over time they quietly erode trust. That's why self-awareness isn't a luxury—it's a necessity. Staying self-aware and course correcting in real time is essential for sustaining trust and building truly collaborative, lasting success.

Mastering the Art of Encouraging Mutually Serving Intentions

Adopting mutually serving intentions begins with a mindset shift that comes with heightened awareness of yourself and others. It's about moving from *What's in it for me?* to *What's in it for us?* or from *What do I want to say?* to *What can I learn about them?*

This shift from *me* to *we* reframes trust as a shared responsibility and affirms that everyone benefits when they feel valued, supported, and seen. Before your next conversation, meeting, or collaboration, take a moment to reflect on your intentions by asking:

- *What interests are being expressed?*

- *What can I offer to support others?*

- *What do I hope to gain from this interaction?*

- *How can we create a mutually beneficial outcome?*

When you engage with others with this mindset, you not only build trust—you lay the foundation for lasting, meaningful relationships. Trust isn't simply earned; it's intentionally built, nurtured, and shared.

While it's natural *and necessary* to consider your own needs, mutually serving intentions call for a balance between what you need and what you can give to others. Your success isn't separate from theirs; it's deeply interconnected.

So, ask yourself: *Do I want to be seen as someone focused only on myself—or as someone who genuinely supports others?* This mindset invites self-awareness and intentionality in how you show up for those around you.

Use these practices to help you master mutually serving intentions:

Foster genuine relationships. Take time to truly know the people you work with. Ask about their experiences, challenges, and insights. Finding common ground strengthens connections and deepens trust.

Encourage open dialogue. Create safe space for honest conversation. Ask about others' goals and how others want to contribute. Listen fully and share your own intentions so that *individual aims* become *shared commitments.*

Share your intentions transparently. Be clear about what you're hoping to achieve—and invite input. Transparency builds mutual respect, reinforcing a sense of purpose and inviting a collaborative spirit.

Ensure clarity and alignment. Confirm shared goals, expectations, and responsibilities. Regular check-ins and a willingness to adapt help foster flexibility and address misalignments early.

Summarize and align on next steps. Close conversations with clarity. Recap agreements and confirm next steps. Proactive follow-up helps build momentum and ensures you're moving forward together—with trust, purpose, and shared ownership.

Practicing mutually serving intentions shifts how you relate, how you lead, and how you show up in the world. It's a quiet force that, over time, transforms moments of interaction into lasting impact.

Keep Agreements

Think of someone you deeply admire—perhaps a mentor, colleague, family member, or friend. What is it about them that earns your trust? Chances are, it's their reliability. They follow through. Their word means something. This quality—keeping agreements—is a cornerstone of trust yet often one of the hardest to consistently uphold.

When you honor your commitments, you reinforce your integrity and earn respect. Reliability builds confidence—not just in others, but in yourself. It's the thread that holds teams, friendships, and families together.

Of course, life gets messy. Deadlines are missed, promises are forgotten, and priorities shift. But trust isn't destroyed by failure—it's compromised when we avoid accountability. The real question is: *How do you respond when things go off track?*

Do you acknowledge the lapse and take ownership? Or do you hope it goes unnoticed, offering excuses that may or may not be believed? Taking responsibility, especially when it's hard, sends a powerful message: *I value this relationship enough to be honest.* That kind of honesty anchors trust and strengthens connection.

Think about how different it feels when someone simply owns their mistake. A thoughtful acknowledgment or sincere apology can soften the impact of a letdown. Being accountable not only repairs trust—it deepens it by showing you care enough to course correct and try again.

The Art of Keeping Agreements

Keeping agreements is about aligning actions with words, demonstrating care and reliability, and showing respect for others' time and needs.

When commitments are repeatedly broken, trust erodes, teams lose momentum, morale declines, and reputations suffer. In relationships, the cost can range from frustration to full disconnection.

But trust isn't built on perfection. Challenges happen. *What matters is how you respond.* When you realize you can't deliver as planned, be proactive. Acknowledge the situation early, take ownership, share what's changed, and propose a path forward. Don't wait until the deadline has passed—initiate the conversation.

Aisha, a respected marketing strategist, was leading a major rebranding effort—but as deadlines passed, she went silent. Despite reassuring the team she was nearly done, her work never materialized. Frustration grew, the project stalled, and team members scrambled to fill the gaps, resulting in inconsistencies that weakened the campaign.

The issue wasn't the missed deadline—it was the lack of communication. Had Aisha spoken up about her challenges, the team could have adapted. Trust wasn't broken by the delay, but by avoidance.

Teams thrive on reliability, and trust is maintained through transparency, accountability, and honest conversations. This is the art of keeping agreements. Once broken, trust is far harder to rebuild than it is to preserve.

What matters most is remembering that revisiting agreements isn't a failure—it's a responsibility. It protects trust by honoring the relationship and your own integrity. Expressing vulnerability—like admitting when you're stuck, that a family matter requires your attention, or that you need to adjust—doesn't invite disappointment; it opens the doors to problem-solving.

In our experience working with thousands of people, trust rarely breaks from unmet agreements alone. It breaks when truth is avoided—when someone stays silent instead of having the honest conversation about what happened. Owning the need for more time, support, or a different approach creates space for collaboration instead of crisis. Nothing erodes trust faster than a broken promise followed by a cover-up.

Prioritizing reliability inspires accountability in others—and fosters a culture where trust isn't just practiced; it's expected.

Mastering the Art of Keeping Agreements

Keeping agreements is about more than just delivering results—it's about how you show up along the way. When you act with intention, communicate openly, and take responsibility, you reinforce trust and demonstrate integrity.

Trust grows in the small moments—one promise, one follow-through at a time. Every commitment you make is a chance to build connection and show others you're someone they can count on. Ultimately, trust isn't just in the doing—it's in the being. It's a reflection of your character.

Keeping your word isn't about perfection—it's about presence. Trust isn't lost with every misstep. When breakdowns happen—and they will—it's how you respond that matters. With honesty and care, even a broken agreement can become a turning point that deepens trust.

Learning to keep your word starts with one powerful practice: pausing. That quiet check-in with yourself can change everything. Before you commit, look inward. *What am I truly agreeing to? Am I clear on what's expected? Do I have the space to deliver?* That moment of reflection isn't hesitation—it's wisdom.

In fact, trust is built over time—and when breakdowns are addressed with honesty and care, they can even strengthen relationships.

Once you've committed, stay connected. Don't drift into silence or let assumptions take the lead. Trust thrives in active communication. Clarify expectations, check in, and keep the conversation alive. Sometimes, a simple alignment can turn confusion into connection.

And when it's time to deliver, follow through with intention. Let your actions reflect your value. If something shifts—and sometimes it will—communicate early. Responsibility isn't just about getting things done; it's about honoring the relationships in the process.

Keeping agreements isn't about being perfect. It's about showing up with clarity, humility, and heart. One promise at a time.

Be Consistent

Imagine a peer who, no matter the situation, consistently keeps their promises, treats others fairly, and behaves predictably—someone whose actions match their words. Now imagine someone whose behavior shifts with their mood or external pressure. Who would you trust more? The answer is clear: *the consistent person.*

Without consistency, even good intentions can fall flat, but consistency doesn't mean rigidity—it means aligning your actions with your values and commitments. Being dependable provides stability in an unpredictable world, allowing trust to grow.

The saying "You're only as trustworthy as your last behavior" reminds us that trust is built not on words but on a steady pattern of reliable actions. Ask yourself: *Do my actions reflect my values? Can others count on me?*

When someone is encouraging one day and dismissive the next, it creates confusion and mistrust. Over time, that unpredictability erodes connection and leaves others unsure of where they stand.

At a fast-paced consulting firm, Rosie and Ben led very differently. Rosie was consistent and dependable—her team trusted her to follow through, even under pressure. Ben, on the other hand, was unpredictable—supportive one day, checked out the next—leaving his team uncertain and disengaged.

When a critical project hit, Rosie's team thrived with clarity and confidence. Ben's team faltered, unsure of his priorities.

The takeaway? Trust isn't built on occasional reliability—it's earned through consistent, steady actions that reflect your values, especially when they count most.

The Art of Being Consistent

Predictability and reliability create a sense of safety.

When people behave consistently, creative energy can be directed toward progress and collaboration—instead of managing uncertainty or guessing how someone will show up today. Consistency frees people to focus forward, fueling creativity, engagement, and growth. In contrast, erratic behavior drains energy, puts people on the defense, and stifles innovation and trust.

During times of change—whether personal or organizational—consistency becomes even more vital. It offers stability when everything else feels uncertain. Leaders who remain calm, fair, and dependable under pressure help their teams stay grounded, resilient, and focused.

Research shows that inconsistent behavior often arises from stress, competing priorities, procrastination, or external pressure. Staying steady during it all demands more than discipline—it calls for inner alignment. It means tuning in to what's driving your reactions, noticing when you're veering off course, and reconnecting with what matters most. This kind of inner clarity allows you to stay grounded and adaptable, even when circumstances are turbulent. It's how you remain anchored in your values while moving with life's inevitable shifts.

To reflect on your own consistency, ask yourself:

- *Do my actions align with the person I aspire to be?*

- *Where do I struggle to remain steady?*

- *How can I improve my consistency to better serve and support others?*

Mastering the Art of Being Consistent

It begins with something simple: doing what you say you'll do. Whether it's following through on a promise or meeting a small deadline, your actions match your words—and people notice. Bit by bit, those moments add up. Trust grows, not with dramatic gestures, but with steady follow-through.

Over time, people come to know they can count on you to come through and understand what to expect from you. Even when pressure builds or plans shift, you remain grounded. You don't have to be perfect—but you are present, predictable, and steady. That dependability becomes part of how others experience you—and how you experience yourself.

At the heart of it all is alignment. You act not from habit alone, but from values that guide your choices. You don't just say what matters to you—you live it. And in doing so, you show others that consistency isn't rigid or robotic. It's a reflection of integrity, intention, and inner clarity.

This is the quiet power of consistency. It's how trust is built—not all at once, but one choice at a time. Draw upon these anchors to master the art of consistency:

Say it. Do it. Align your actions with your words—trust grows with follow-through.

Be steady, not perfect. Show up predictably, even under pressure—consistency builds credibility.

Live your values. Let your behavior reflect what you stand for—authenticity earns trust.

Consistency is the quiet foundation of trust—built not through perfection, but through steady, values-driven follow-through. It begins with honoring your word in small ways and grows as your actions reliably reflect your intentions. Over time, others learn they can count on you—not because you're flawless, but because you're grounded, present, and aligned with what you stand for. This kind of integrity isn't rigid; it's authentic, intentional, and deeply human. One choice at a time, consistency becomes your credibility.

This is the power of Trust of Character. It's your internal compass—proven through consistent, values-aligned action. When it is present, people follow through, boundaries are respected, expectations are clear, and intentions are shared. Teams operate with purpose, individuals know how to support one another, and relationships remain steady—even in uncertainty. Trust of Character is what makes alignment possible, collaboration real, and integrity visible.

Trust of Character lays the foundation—but it's only the beginning. Once people know they can rely on each other's actions, the door opens for deeper dialogue. Trust of Communication, which you will explore in the next chapter, begins to take shape through your openness, honesty, and courage to speak—and hear—the truth.

CHAPTER THREE

Trust of Communication

The Power of Openness and Honesty

> *Honesty and transparency make you vulnerable.*
> *Be honest and transparent anyway.*
> MOTHER TERESA

Trust of Character lays the foundation for alignment, synergy, and purpose in relationships, teamwork, and direction. Trust of Communication builds on that foundation with openness, honesty, and transparency—creating a space where it's safe to be fully human.[1]

> *Ava sat in the conference room, her stomach in knots as her team struggled through a flawed project plan. She had spotted the issues weeks ago—misaligned priorities, missing data, unclear goals—and had raised concerns, only to be dismissed.*
>
> *Now, as the cracks became undeniable, her manager asked, "Why didn't anyone flag this earlier?" Ava hesitated. She could have spoken up again, but the damage was already done. Trust had been eroded—not because she hadn't seen the problems, but because she hadn't been heard.*

This is the power—and the peril—of communication. When truth is left unspoken, concerns unheard, and assumptions unchecked, trust unravels. It's not just about deadlines or data; it's about trust in communication itself.

Consider your own experiences:

- *Have you ever felt the pain of being misunderstood?*

- *Have others made false assumptions about you and acted on them without verification?*

- *Have you been dismissed as the messenger delivering difficult news?*

- *Have you had to make critical decisions, only to later realize that essential information was withheld?*

Whether at work or at home, communication gaps, misunderstandings, and unverified assumptions create daily disconnects that damage morale, hinder collaboration, and erode trust. Trust in communication shapes every interaction—it determines how openly we share, how we extend trust, and how deeply we connect with others.

When built on trust, communication fosters collaboration, strengthens relationships, and creates psychological safety, allowing people to address challenges together. It ensures shared understanding, mutual respect, and a clear sense of where we stand with one another. Without trust, communication falters, misunderstandings arise, and progress stalls.

Trust in communication empowers us to exchange critical information, own our mistakes, and navigate challenges with honesty and care. It's more than just an exchange of words; it's a connection that bridges head and heart, fostering stronger, more authentic relationships that fuel collaboration and meaningful impact. That's why in this chapter, we will explore the six behaviors that effectively build Trust of Communication:

- Share information.

- Tell the truth.

- Admit mistakes.

- Give and receive constructive feedback.

- Maintain confidentiality.

- Speak with good purpose.

Trust of Communication (figure 6) shapes how people talk openly, honestly, and transparently with one another. By practicing its six core behaviors, you unlock the potential to build stronger, more resilient relationships while understanding yourself and others more deeply.

Let's dive deeper into the behaviors and discover how each can transform the way you communicate and lead.

Figure 6. Trust of Communication

Share Information

Open, honest, and transparent communication is at the heart of Trust of Communication. Most of us know how important it is to share information—but in practice, it often falls short. And when it does, it can quietly derail progress and strain even the strongest relationships. When information flows freely, it builds confidence, fuels collaboration, and helps people move forward with clarity. But when it's withheld—*or just perceived to be withheld*—frustration grows, morale dips, and teamwork starts to unravel.

This kind of breakdown is especially tough during times of change: strategic shifts, evolving roles, or new priorities. When people are kept in the dark, they don't just feel excluded—they feel blindsided. Energy gets directed toward managing confusion, instead of focusing on solutions. And the moment someone realizes others had information that they didn't?! That doesn't just sting—it can trigger a withdrawal of trust.

Lisa, a rising star in her company's operations department, eagerly took on a high-stakes project. She meticulously planned every detail, confident in her strategy. But as the project unfolded, unexpected challenges, supply delays, budget cuts, and shifting leadership priorities began to surface.

Her manager, James, had known about these risks from executive meetings but chose not to share them. He assumed shielding Lisa from the complexity would help her stay focused. Instead, it left her unaware of the realities she needed to navigate. The project faltered. Trust frayed.

Had James communicated early, Lisa could have adjusted, led with clarity, and brought her team along with confidence. Instead, his silence created confusion and ultimately left her scrambling and her team disillusioned.

The lesson? Information isn't just power—it's the currency of trust. When shared, it fosters unity and aligned action. When withheld, even unintentionally, it creates distance and doubt.

The Art of Sharing Information

Our research shows that the biggest barriers to sharing information often stem from fear of losing status, expertise, or control. Some worry that once they share what they know, they will lose their edge. But withholding information weakens trust, stalls collaboration, and ultimately costs valuable opportunities.

People withhold information for these main reasons:

Confidentiality: Protecting sensitive data is essential, but it requires clarity. *What can be shared? What can't?* When this is not clear, silence becomes the default.

Fear of losing control: Especially during uncertain times, some people hold back information to feel secure. But this self-protection often undermines team cohesion and transparency.

Simple oversight: Sometimes, it's not intentional—it's just forgetting to share or assuming others already know. But even unintentional silence can lead to breakdowns in trust.

The antidote? Proactive communication. The more intentional we are about sharing what we know, the more we reduce friction, strengthen alignment, and foster trust.

Mastering the Art of Sharing Information

Sharing information isn't just a mindset—it's a practice. Make transparency a daily habit with these simple actions:

Schedule intentional check-ins. Don't wait for information to surface on its own. Build routines that encourage open updates.

Ask: *Who needs to know? When? What context do they need to succeed?*

Deliver information thoughtfully. Tailor your message to the situation and the person. Choose the right tone, timing, and level of detail. Sharing isn't just about what you say—it's about how others receive it.

Encourage dialogue. Make space for questions. Invite clarification. Transparency isn't one way—it's a two-way conversation. Dialogue deepens understanding and reinforces shared purpose.

Keeping people informed isn't just practical—it's personal. Sharing information shows respect, builds confidence, and invites others to step in with clarity and purpose. When in doubt, communicate more, not less. When people are informed and engaged, they stop guessing—and start trusting. That's the power of shared information.

Tell the Truth

Honest communication is one of the most courageous acts in any relationship—yet it often begins with a quiet, internal pause. Ask yourself:

- *Am I fully transparent, or do I sometimes hold back to avoid discomfort?*

- *Do I soften the truth to prevent conflict?*

- *Have I stayed silent out of fear of judgment?*

- *Do I say what I believe others want to hear instead of what I truly feel?*

These aren't questions of blame—they're invitations to self-awareness. The more clearly you see your patterns, the more intentional you can be about the choices you make in how you show up and behave.

But as we all know, telling the truth isn't always easy. Fear of judgment, lost opportunities, or being sidelined often tempts us to offer partial truths, "white lies," or to withhold key information. But even half-truths or omissions can create confusion and distance.

If you've ever sensed someone wasn't telling you the whole story or you needed to fact-check after a conversation, you've felt the impact: trust erodes, momentum stalls, and relationships suffer.

The lesson? Even when uncomfortable, honest communication strengthens relationships, accelerates alignment, and creates space for real solutions. The more truth is spoken, the more trust is reinforced.

The Art of Telling the Truth

Let's face it, it takes a quiet courage to communicate honestly—especially when the truth feels uncomfortable. You might worry about being judged, being criticized, or harming a relationship. Maybe you're unsure if the other person is ready—*or willing*—to hear your perspective. It is tempting to soften or filter the truth to make it easier to hear or say. But trust is not built on comfort. It's built on authenticity—the kind that honors both the truth and the relationship.

These guiding principles will help you practice the art of telling the truth:

Be compassionate with yourself. Recognize that your truth is shaped from your unique lived experiences. Honor that. Give yourself grace when sharing it, even if it feels uncomfortable.

Honest expression not only builds trust with others—it builds trust within yourself.

Speak with courage and care. Telling the truth may feel risky, but thoughtful honesty earns lasting respect. People can sense when you are being authentic. Over time, your courage to speak openly deepens trust and connection.

Take ownership. Trust doesn't start at the top—it starts with you. When your words and actions align with honesty, you lead by example. Owning your truth helps create a culture where integrity is the norm and trust can thrive—at work, at home, and in every relationship.

When you lead with honesty, grounded in courage and personal responsibility, you create the conditions for trust to take root. It's in these moments that relationships grow stronger, more resilient, and deeply real. By embracing honesty, courage, and responsibility, you lay the foundation for relationships rooted in trust. Telling the truth isn't just a skill—it's a way of being that allows everyone involved to thrive, including you.

Mastering the Art of Telling the Truth

Mastery begins not with perfection; it begins with intention. It starts with the choice to pause and check in with yourself before speaking—to ask, *What do I really believe? What needs to be said?* It's the courage to show up as your full self, even when you feel vulnerable, and the grace to stay open to other perspectives while sharing your own.

In practice, this looks like

- **Starting with clarity:** *What I know to be true . . . ,* before sharing emotions or interpretations.

- **Framing your perspective with humility:** *Here's how I see it . . .*

- **Creating dialogue:** *Can I share how I'm experiencing this?* and/or *How do you see it?*

- **Naming discomfort:** *This is hard for me to say, but it matters.*

- **Allowing feelings to surface without apology:** *I am having difficulty understanding . . .*

- **Checking for understanding:** *I'd like to check for understanding before we part ways.*

Telling the truth isn't about being blunt or being right—it's about being real. And in relationships built on truth, trust doesn't just grow. It transforms.

Admit Mistakes

Growth—whether personal or organizational—requires risk.

To grow, either in life or in business, you must be willing to step into the unknown, to take risks. The truth is, sometimes those risks pay off. Other times, they fall short. But it's in those moments—when plans don't go as expected or hoped—that our greatest growth can unfold. That's part of life's journey.

Mistakes might feel like setbacks, but they're invitations to learn, adjust, and evolve. The biggest leaps and breakthroughs in life don't come from getting everything right; they come from taking a leap, stumbling, and discovering something deeper on the way.

Our personal growth and evolution come not from perfection, but from reflecting on (and learning from) our mistakes. Mistakes, in this way, are part of the human experience. They're not detours from the path—they *are* the path.

In fact, many of the most innovative people and businesses are often propelled forward, not despite mistakes, but because of them. While risk-taking, creativity, and innovation are encouraged, mistakes are inevitable. Some organizations even welcome them as necessary fuel for innovation.

> *Take Sara Blakely, founder of Spanx. When she was growing up, her father would regularly ask at the dinner table, "What did you fail at today?"—reframing failure as a sign of effort and growth. If she hadn't failed at something, he considered it a missed opportunity to stretch beyond her comfort zone. That question changed everything. It helped Sara learn early that failure isn't something to fear—it's a teacher and a stepping stone. It's a natural part of learning, improving, and ultimately succeeding, and it's a sign that you're on the edge of something new.*

Armed with that mindset, turning mistakes into learning opportunities, Sara went on to build a billion-dollar business with no formal background in fashion or entrepreneurship. Her success wasn't about avoiding mistakes; it was about using them to build resilience, insight, and self-trust.

Mistakes can happen for all kinds of reasons—bad timing, misreading the market, underestimating the effort required, or simple human error. What matters most is what comes next in how you respond. *Do you deflect, hide, or blame? Or do you acknowledge, reflect, and take responsibility?*

Your response to your own mistakes and to the mistakes of others says everything about the level of trust, compassion, and accountability you're willing to bring to the table. When someone owns their misstep, you have a choice: you can punish them, or you can honor the courage it took to admit it—and move forward together.

In truth, owning mistakes is one of the most powerful ways to build trust. It sends a message that says: *I'm not here to be perfect—I'm here to grow, support others, and stay in integrity.* That mindset strengthens teams, deepens relationships, and fuels lasting success.

Owning mistakes—not only your own but also encouraging others to do the same—is one of the most powerful ways to build trust, show support, and foster accountability. When done well, it fuels learning, strengthens teams, and drives lasting success, whether in business or in personal relationships.

The Art of Admitting Mistakes

Mistakes are not evidence of failure—they're reminders that we're human, learning and evolving. And yet, it's tempting to hide them. We fear being judged, losing credibility, or disappointing others. But avoiding accountability often causes more damage than the mistake itself.

Owning a misstep doesn't reduce your worth. In fact, it reveals self-awareness, strength, and an honest commitment to growth. When you respond to your own mistakes with compassion, you reinforce the truth that learning—*not perfection*—is the real goal.

Environments that blend accountability with empathy foster greater trust, creativity, and connection. People feel safer to take risks, to stretch, to speak up. When we normalize mistake making as part of learning, we liberate ourselves—and others—from the myth of perfection.

As Maya Angelou once said, *Forgive yourself for not knowing what you didn't know before you learned it.*[2] Mistakes are not the end of the story—they're often the beginning of something better.

Consider Thomas Edison, who famously reframed over a thousand failures as steps on the path to success. His resilience reminds us: every mistake, when owned and explored, holds a lesson or an opportunity.

The takeaway? Owning your mistakes cultivates honesty, humility, and stronger communication—and inspires others to do the same. In doing so, you create healthier teams, deeper relationships, and a culture grounded in trust.

Mastering the Art of Admitting Mistakes

When you've made a mistake, here's how to move through it with integrity and grace.

Acknowledge and own it. Face your mistake with courage. Choose honesty over avoidance. Take responsibility for what happened, clearly, directly, and without blame. Recognize the impact and apologize. A sincere apology isn't weakness—it's the foundation of trust.

Assess and adjust. Use reflection as a tool to turn regret into growth. Ask yourself: *What happened? Why?* Then, refine your approach. When you identify the cause and make meaningful changes, mistakes become turning points.

Learn and move forward. Bring self-compassion into the learning process. Reframe setbacks as lessons. When others see you grow from your missteps, it gives them permission to do the same. By learning and applying what you discover, you deepen your trustworthiness and inspire growth in those around you.

We all stumble. But what builds trust isn't perfection—it's ownership. Admitting mistakes with humility opens the door to learning, repairing, and deepening respect, where people feel free to show up fully—flaws and all.

Give and Receive Constructive Feedback

When it comes to feedback, there are two primary types that build trust, both of which are essential for clarity, growth, and alignment:

- **Positive reinforcement:** Recognizes and celebrates strengths and acknowledges how one's behavior is supporting positive results

- **Constructive critique**: Offers helpful guidance by pointing out areas for growth and identifying opportunities for improvement

While feedback is often associated with job performance, when it comes to trust building, its impact extends far beyond tasks. Feedback provides insight into how you are perceived, how your behavior aligns with your intentions, and how your behavior may unknowingly affect trust in your relationships. Our research shows that over 90 percent of trust breakdowns result from misunderstandings, misalignment, or unconscious missteps, rather than intentional harm.[3] By engaging in open and constructive feedback, you can address these gaps and create opportunities for mutual growth.

But giving feedback can feel risky.

You may worry about how it will be received, whether it will be taken personally, or if it will create conflict or even lead to retaliation in low-trust environments. The fear of damaging a relationship can make it tempting to stay silent. On the other side, receiving feedback can stir up emotion, defensiveness, or self-doubt. No one likes feeling like they've missed the mark. But avoiding feedback only prevents self-awareness, limiting personal and relational growth. When concerns go unspoken, trust erodes, issues linger, and collaboration begins to break down.

The Art of Constructive Feedback

During a team meeting, Maya noticed that her colleague Jake often interrupted quieter team members. Wanting to address it constructively, she pulled him aside and said, "Can I share an observation with you?"

She explained, "I've noticed you sometimes jump in quickly during discussions. I know you're passionate, but it is harder for others to contribute. I'm bringing it up because I know you value collaboration."

Jake paused, reflected, and responded, "I hadn't realized that. Thanks for letting me know—I'll be more mindful moving forward."

The key to giving effective feedback is thoughtful preparation and clear intention. When feedback is offered with the goal of fostering growth and awareness, it becomes an act of service. In Maya's case, by focusing on shared values and improvement—not criticism—she helped Jake recognize his behavior without triggering his defensiveness.

Before offering feedback, take a moment to reflect on your intentions. The goal should always be to help the other person grow and gain perspective and to strengthen the relationship.

Managing your emotions is essential, so approach the conversation calmly, aiming for mutual understanding, rather than blame.

A respectful way to start is by asking permission: *Is this a good time to share some observations?* This signals respect, ensures the person is receptive, and creates a safe space for dialogue. It also shows that your feedback is meant to support—not criticize.

Once permission is given, describe the behavior objectively and specifically: *During our meeting last week, I noticed . . .* Focus on facts, not assumptions. Avoid charged language like *You always* or *You never*, which can trigger defensiveness. Keeping the tone constructive encourages openness and collaboration.

After sharing, invite their perspective by asking: *How can we work together to improve this?* This shifts the conversation from blame to shared responsibility and problem-solving. Expressing gratitude for their openness also reinforces trust, helping feedback become a positive, empowering experience, rather than a negative one.

Mastering the Art of Constructive Feedback

When given and received with care, constructive feedback strengthens trust. It fosters open communication, mutual respect, and shared understanding while creating opportunities to deepen connection, enhance collaboration, and build a culture of continuous growth.

Remember, feedback is about *progress—rather than perfection.* When you approach it with courage, compassion, and a willingness to learn, you strengthen relationships and create space for meaningful improvement. And remember that receiving feedback with openness and grace is just as powerful as giving it.

Consider the following tips for *receiving feedback* with courage and grace:

Stay open. Assume positive intent, and trust that feedback is meant to support your growth. Manage emotional reactions—pause, breathe, and listen with curiosity, rather than defensiveness.

Seek understanding. Ask clarifying questions to ensure you understand the heart of the feedback. Summarize what you're hearing and invite collaboration on solutions. Show appreciation for the effort and honesty with a simple "thank you."

Reflect and apply. Give yourself space to reflect before reacting. Ask: *What can I learn? How can I grow stronger from this?* Thoughtful reflection turns feedback into lasting improvement.

Check out these tips for *giving feedback* with compassion:

Lead with compassion. Think of yourself as a guide, not a critic. Frame feedback as a gift to build confidence, raise awareness, and inspire growth.

Focus on behavior, not character. Address specific actions *without* making it personal. Protect the relationship by speaking to behaviors, not labels.

Give feedback promptly. Share insights while they're fresh, meaningful, and actionable. It's just like planting seeds in fertile soil, which provides the best chance for growth.

Feedback, when given with care, is a gift. It helps us grow, stay aligned, and strengthen relationships. Offering it thoughtfully—and receiving it with openness—keeps communication honest and trust alive.

Maintain Confidentiality

Whether in personal relationships or professional environments, maintaining confidentiality safeguards sensitive information and preserves trust. How you handle what's shared with you determines the trust others place in you.

Honoring confidentiality is more than a virtue—it's a core expression of integrity that fosters security and anchors strong relationships. Being entrusted with private information is a privilege that carries real responsibility, but a breach, intentional or not, can damage relationships and erode trust. When confidentiality is respected, it builds a culture of mutual respect, reliability, and lasting connection.

The Art of Maintaining Confidentiality

Confidentiality is the cornerstone of trust. When we protect sensitive information—whether it's a workplace decision, a job promotion, a life change, a personal struggle, or a health concern—we create a space where people feel safe to share openly. Being entrusted with confidential information shows that others see you as reliable, and it helps strengthen mutual respect.

But the flip side is just as important. Breaking confidentiality—whether through gossip, speculation, or careless sharing—can quickly unravel trust. It doesn't always come from a bad place, but even well-meaning conversations with blurry boundaries can cause harm. Trust is delicate, and once it's broken, it's tough to rebuild.

Confidentiality isn't just a workplace standard—it matters just as much in our personal lives. When someone shares something deeply personal or vulnerable, they're letting you into their world and trusting you to keep it safe. That story belongs to them, not you.

At the heart of it, confidentiality isn't only about what you don't say—it's about how you honor the trust someone has placed in you. When you protect what's been shared, you're showing integrity, respect, and care—and that's how trust stays strong.

Mastering the Art of Maintaining Confidentiality

Mastering confidentiality requires deliberate, daily choices to honor the trust others have placed in you. Here are ways to maintain confidentiality:

Be clear about what's private. If something needs to stay confidential, state it as so. When others share something sensitive, treat it as private unless explicitly told otherwise.

Respect the trust you're given. Handle personal and professional information with care. Don't use it to boost your image or gain an advantage.

Don't gossip. Even casual conversations about private matters can break trust. If you wouldn't say it with the person present, don't say it at all.

When in doubt, don't share. If you're unsure whether something is OK to share, ask first. Respect and intention matter most.

Being trusted with information is an honor—and a responsibility. Protecting confidentiality reinforces psychological safety and shows others they can count on your integrity, even when no one's watching.

Speak with Good Purpose

During a team meeting, Marcus hesitated before shar-
ing his idea. Unsure how it would be received, he took a
breath and began to speak—only to be cut off by Lisa's
smirk and a muttered "Here we go again." A few team
members chuckled, and Marcus, feeling dismissed and
embarrassed, fell silent.

Later, Lisa and a colleague gossiped about him in the
break room. "Marcus always rambles," Lisa said, laughing.
When word reached Marcus, his frustration gave way to
quiet resignation. He stopped offering ideas altogether.

In the weeks that followed, the team faced mounting chal-
lenges—the very problems Marcus had ideas to solve. With-
out his contributions, creativity stalled, solutions dried up,
and the project fell short of expectations. Leadership soon
questioned why no new ideas had emerged.

The lesson was unmistakable: a few moments of sarcasm, gossip, and dismissiveness had silenced a valuable voice. In doing so, the team weakened trust, stifled collaboration, and eroded the very cohesion they needed to succeed.

Have you ever found yourself in a similar situation?

Maybe you've been hurt by gossip—or perhaps, without realizing it, you've participated in it. Gossip is one of the most subtle yet powerful forces that can chip away at trust, especially during times of change and uncertainty. It often arises when speculation takes hold: *Who might lose their job? Who could be promoted? When will the reorg happen?*

Life inevitably brings uncertainty when you feel doubt, frustration, or fear, or when things just don't go the way you had hoped. In those moments, you have a choice: get swept up in assumptions and negativity—or pause and choose to speak with intention and good purpose.

Speaking with good purpose means caring enough about the relationship to be honest and direct, guided by respect and positive intent. It's especially important when something feels off—when words or actions are unclear, or emotions run high. This kind of communication helps you stay grounded in respect, strengthens connection, and protects trust when it matters most.

When you speak with clarity, care, and purpose, you create space for real understanding and meaningful dialogue. That is how trust grows. In contrast, things like gossip, sarcasm, and brushing people off quietly chip away at trust and create distance.

At its core, intentional communication isn't just a skill—it's a conscious choice to let your words reflect your values. When you do that, you build stronger relationships, encourage collaboration, and grow into a more self-aware, trustworthy version of yourself.

The Art of Speaking with Good Purpose

Speaking with good purpose means communicating with clarity, authenticity, and empathy. It's about aligning your words with your values—saying what you mean and doing so with respect. Instead of talking about someone, you speak directly to them. This kind of intentional communication builds trust, bridges misunderstandings, and creates a culture where openness and collaboration can thrive.

On the other hand, careless communication—like gossip, sarcasm, or indirect criticism—undermines trust. Gossip can damage reputations, raise doubts about your integrity, and make others hesitant to confide in you. And, while venting can offer temporary relief, without a constructive path forward, it often fuels negativity and stalls progress.

> *After a long day, Lena approached Malik, hoping to clear the air. She had noticed his frustration in meetings and wanted to explain the problems she was having with the new reporting tool.*
>
> *But as she stood there, doubt crept in: "What if he doesn't listen? What if it makes things worse? Maybe it's not worth it."*
>
> *Malik glanced up from his phone, clearly distracted. Lena hesitated. Instead of speaking up, she paused, forced a polite smile, mumbled a hello, and walked away carrying the weight of frustration and missed connection.*
>
> *Though she sensed the conversation could have helped, fear and doubt kept her silent. Without realizing it, both Lena and Malik missed an opportunity to clear the air, build on understanding, and take a step forward in trust.*

In moments of tension, it's easy to stay silent. Fear, doubt, and discomfort often block us from speaking with good purpose. People give the following reasons for holding back:

- *I've already tried.* It didn't help before—so why try again?

- *I'm too frustrated.* It feels like others should get it by now, and patience is running low.

- *I won't be heard.* Worry about being dismissed, misunderstood, or rejected creates hesitation.

- *I'm not even sure I'm right.* When emotions feel tangled, it's hard to trust what you're feeling.

- *I don't want to make it worse.* Speaking up might lead to more tension—or even backlash.

- *I don't know how to say it.* The right words feel just out of reach, so you say nothing.

These feelings are real—and you're not alone in experiencing them. But with practice and intention, you can find your voice and speak in ways that strengthen trust, connection, and clarity.

Mastering the Art of Speaking with Good Purpose

Mastering the art of speaking with good purpose requires both inner reflection and intentional action. And together, these elements work to create meaningful, respectful conversations that strengthen trust.

Trust in communication isn't automatic—it's earned through honesty, courage, and thoughtful intention, one conversation at a time. Every interaction matters.

Whether you're sharing information openly, speaking your truth with courage, admitting mistakes, giving or receiving feedback with care, protecting confidentiality, or choosing your words with purpose, each moment either builds or erodes trust.

The way we communicate each day—especially in moments that matter—shapes the trust we build over time. To create the kind of environment where trust can truly take root, consider your own internal preparation of cultivating mindfulness:

Name what you feel. Reflect on your emotions and the reasons behind them. Naming your feelings brings clarity and helps you respond thoughtfully, not impulsively.

Claim your experience. Acknowledge your emotions without judgment. Validating what you feel gives you the power to communicate intentionally rather than reactively.

Reframe your mindset. Shift from blame to empowerment by focusing on solutions rather than problems. Remember: the impact of someone's actions doesn't always match their intent. Staying objective keeps the conversation grounded.

To help foster real connection and fuel healthy collaboration, consider how you might build connection during external engagements:

Start with clear intentions. Open by sharing why you're speaking up: *I want to discuss this to better understand your perspective and strengthen our relationship.*

Invite dialogue and listen. Ask open-ended questions to create space for conversation: *How do you see this situation? What are your thoughts?*

Speak honestly and build solutions. Use *I* statements to express your experience without blame, then collaborate on next steps: *I felt concerned when this happened because it impacted our timeline. How can we move forward together?*

How we speak matters just as much as what we say. Speaking with good purpose means choosing words that respect, uplift, and clarify—or challenge constructively when needed. It's a conscious choice to communicate in ways that build trust, not break it—because trust lives in every conversation.

But trust doesn't stop with how we speak—it also lives in how we *see* one another. Trust of Capability, which you will explore in the next chapter, begins when we recognize each other's strengths, support growth, and create space for people to rise to their full potential.

CHAPTER FOUR

Trust of Capability
Empowering Growth and Contribution

Most discussions of decision making assume
that only senior executives make decisions or
that only executives' decisions matter.
This is a dangerous mistake.
PETER F. DRUCKER

Trust of Capability begins with believing in people—their strengths, their potential, and their ability to contribute meaningfully.[1] It's about creating space for others to step up, grow, and thrive.

Have you ever felt like your skills and experience were being overlooked—like you weren't trusted to do what you're capable of? Maybe you've worked hard to prove yourself, yet you find your contributions undervalued. It's frustrating when you know you have more to offer, but you feel held back—by systems, assumptions, or someone else's control.

On the other side, you may have worked with someone whose approach made collaboration difficult. A colleague who dismisses ideas, takes over tasks, or shuts down teamwork, unintentionally

79

holding things back instead of moving them forward. Arnold was one of those people.

> *Arnold was brilliant and deeply experienced. He prided himself on being the expert—but his need for control came at a cost. Rather than empowering his team, he insisted on doing everything himself, convinced it was the only way to ensure quality and efficiency. Instead, progress stalled, innovation faded, and frustration grew. The standard becomes survival, not excellence.*
>
> *Eager to contribute, team members found themselves constantly waiting—waiting for tasks to be delegated, for their ideas to be heard, and for a real chance to use their skills. Over time, enthusiasm gave way to disengagement. Some moved on. Others checked out. As morale dropped, so did the team's performance and reputation.*

What Arnold didn't see was this: collaboration isn't about being the smartest person in the room—it's about creating space for everyone to contribute. Trust of Capability isn't just about what you know. It's about fostering an environment where people are encouraged to take ownership, empowered to contribute, and able to expand their potential. When people are trusted with meaningful responsibilities, they rise. When they're not, they retreat—or leave.

Arnold's story isn't unique. In teams and organizations everywhere, growth is often blocked not by lack of talent, but by micromanagement, withholding, or failing to recognize people's strengths. *The good news? These patterns can change.*

When we practice Trust of Capability, we can create environments where people feel empowered to step up, contribute fully, and develop their best selves. It's not only about recognizing your own skills—it's about seeing and valuing the strengths of others. When you do, you invite diverse perspectives, strengthen collaboration, and unlock shared learning and results.

Yes, your knowledge matters. But Trust of Capability goes beyond subject-matter expertise. It's reflected in how you build relationships, seek out different viewpoints, and respect the lived experiences others bring to the table. In today's interconnected world, where success depends on working across diverse teams, cultures, and backgrounds, this quality of trust isn't optional—it's essential.

When people feel trusted for what they bring—and believed in for who they can become—they show up more confident, committed, and connected. Thriving teams aren't built on individual brilliance alone. They're shaped by a shared mindset: one rooted in humility, learning, and a deep curiosity for growth.

Extending trust empowers people to step forward, share their perspectives, and take ownership of their impact. It invites smart risk-taking, sparks innovation, and fuels momentum. Growth becomes a shared journey—one everyone is invested in.

You see Trust of Capability show up in everyday actions. You see it in teams that ask questions, embrace dialogue, and welcome curiosity. You see it in leaders and peers who embody trust and don't micromanage, who support others and value their input, and who believe in their teams' ability to move forward—together.

Most importantly, Trust of Capability isn't just about who people are today—it's about believing in who they can become. This kind of trust builds resilience, readiness, and long-term success.

At its heart, Trust of Capability is about acknowledging and empowering potential—your own and others'. When people feel seen and valued for what they bring, they go beyond expectations. They lead, innovate, and uplift others. That's how you build a culture of shared success.

To make Trust of Capability real and actionable, we focus on four core behaviors:

- Acknowledge people's skills and abilities.

- Empower people to make decisions.

- Involve others and seek their input.

- Help people learn skills.

Building and sustaining Trust of Capability (figure 7) requires daily, intentional effort. It means actively investing in your own growth while supporting the growth and development of others. But growth cannot be delegated—it starts within you. When you commit to learning and creating space for others to do the same, you cultivate an environment where everyone feels confident, capable, and ready to contribute.

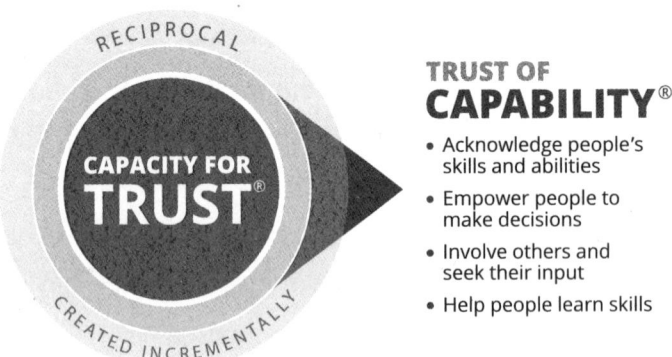

Figure 7. Trust of Capability

Without that foundation, people retreat into their own lanes. Energy fades, morale drops, and progress stalls, the lowest common denominator becoming the norm. The standard becomes survival, not excellence. It's clear: where trust is absent, growth slows; but where trust is present, potential is unlocked, momentum builds, and success becomes a shared journey.

It all begins with a simple but powerful act: acknowledging people's skills and abilities.

Acknowledge People's Skills and Abilities

Across teams, organizations, and relationships, one thing is unilaterally true: people want to feel seen, heard, valued, and acknowledged—not just for completed tasks, but for the unique skills, talents, and perspectives each person brings.

When you genuinely recognize someone's contribution, including their expertise, effort, and heart—you are doing more than showing appreciation. You're fueling their confidence, affirming their value, and deepening their sense of purpose. Your actions say, *What you bring truly matters*, laying the foundation of trust and inspiring people to contribute their best work.

Acknowledgment goes beyond praising outcomes; it's about seeing the person behind the work—who they are—their intentions, generosity, and drive. When you see others fully, you create an environment of respect, encouragement, and empowerment. Sometimes, that recognition helps people discover strengths in themselves they hadn't fully seen before. Take this moment from a team meeting:

Nia proposed a new strategy to streamline workflow. Her colleague Omar scoffed, "I've been doing this for years. That approach won't work," shutting down the conversation and leaving Nia hesitant to contribute further.

Later, teammate David spoke up: "Nia, I appreciate your perspective. You're seeing something we may have overlooked. Let's explore it." By acknowledging her idea and inviting collaboration, David made Nia feel valued and encouraged her continued contributions.

In that moment, David's humility built trust and strengthened collaboration, while Omar's dismissiveness stifled innovation.

The takeaway? Real leadership isn't about having the final word—it's about lifting others up, valuing their contributions, and creating space for growth.

Like any act of generosity, acknowledgment creates a ripple effect. It strengthens trust, fuels collaboration, and empowers people to take risks, explore new ideas, and grow into their potential. When you recognize others' abilities, you help them see their own strengths, creating a foundation for a culture where everyone, including you, can thrive.

The Art of Acknowledging People's Skills and Abilities

Whether in work or in life, the art of acknowledgment is one of the most powerful ways to build trust, ignite collaboration, and unlock potential—not only in others but in yourself. True acknowledgment goes beyond recognizing completed tasks. It's about seeing the whole person—their insight, effort, and energy—as well as the value they bring through their perspective, presence, and potential.

Think about it—you thrive when someone truly sees you. When you extend the same recognition to others, you're actively building Trust of Capability and contributing to an environment where people feel valued, seen, and motivated to make a difference.

This kind of acknowledgment is about more than simply gratitude; it's a profound affirmation of a person's worth. It's not limited to appreciating what someone *does*; it's about honoring who they are. When people feel recognized in this way, they're more likely to take on new challenges, contribute creatively, and grow with confidence. And, in turn, your relationships with them strengthen.

When you acknowledge others' abilities, you're helping them face uncertainty with curiosity, rather than fear. This action-oriented trust also helps you own a sense of trust—in them and in yourself, as a mentor or leader.

Acknowledging people's skills and abilities builds shared confidence. It fosters a culture of mutual trust, innovation, and collaboration—one where people who feel valued are more likely to invest their energy and creativity in their work, which leads to better outcomes for everyone. At its core, acknowledgment fosters shared confidence. It strengthens the trust between individuals and across teams. When people feel seen, they bring more of themselves to their work—more energy, more creativity, more commitment—which leads to stronger outcomes and a more resilient culture.

Trust of Capability thrives in environments where acknowledgment is intentional and sincere, rooted in respect, and drives individual growth and team success. When you master this art, you contribute to an environment where everyone feels empowered to excel. It's the catalyst for individual growth and collective success. When you master this art, you help create a space where people are empowered to stretch, lead, and excel.

Bottom line? Acknowledgment creates a cycle of trust. *What you give to others comes back to you*—ultimately strengthening your belief in your own abilities while reinforcing the bonds of mutual growth and collaboration.

Mastering the Art of Acknowledging People's Skills and Abilities

Effectively acknowledging others' skills and abilities begins with an intentional and genuine mindset. These practices can help you transform acknowledgment from a skill into a natural, everyday *way of being*:

See the person, not just the task. Go beyond appreciating completed work—see and acknowledge the skills, insights, and impact the person brought. Honor their unique experiences and strengths to show that you notice *who* they are as much as what they do. It's about conveying, *I see you, not just your work.*

Express gratitude with heart and specificity. A genuine "thank you" can uplift and inspire. Be specific about what you appreciate—the effort, the creativity, the leadership—so people feel truly seen and motivated to keep growing: *Your calm during that chaotic meeting helped everyone focus.*

Show you believe in their potential. Acknowledgment takes more than words—it takes action. Offer space for people to stretch their talents and take on new challenges and trust them to lead their own success. Believing in someone's potential invites them to rise even higher. It says, *I see something in you, and I know you've got this.*

Authentic acknowledgment builds trust when it's expressed with sincerity and consistency. Make it a regular part of how you lead, collaborate, and connect—not just something reserved for big wins. The more you practice it with intention, the more it becomes woven into your presence and into the culture you help shape.

Empower People to Make Decisions

When Camilla became director of operations, she noticed her team hesitated to make decisions, escalating even minor issues to her. Years of micromanagement had eroded their confidence.

Determined to change the culture, Camilla clearly defined decision-making responsibilities and encouraged her team to trust their judgment. When Mateo hesitated on a vendor decision, she asked, "You know the project's needs best—what's your recommendation?"

At first, the team was nervous, but as Camilla reinforced their choices, offered guidance, and celebrated wins, their confidence grew. Productivity soared, morale improved, and the team became more engaged. By trusting her team to decide, Camilla not only freed up her time—she built a stronger, more capable team.

In today's fast-paced workplaces, the ability to make independent decisions is the foundation of trust, efficiency, and success. Gone are the days of rigid hierarchies where every choice requires top-down approval. Modern teams thrive on collaboration, shared accountability, and trust in each other's expertise. To navigate this landscape, people need both the freedom and confidence to make decisions that impact their work. When it comes to decision-making, ask yourself these questions:

- *Do I give others the freedom to make decisions about their own work?*

- *Do I trust their expertise and judgment to find the right solutions?*

- *Or do I second-guess and overcontrol, becoming a barrier instead of a supporter?*

The way you empower others—or hold them back—shapes the culture of trust within your relationships and team. When you choose to trust people, you give them space to grow, to think outside the box and take on new challenges. They become more engaged, innovative, and creative.

But, if that trust is missing, it's a different story. People can start to doubt their abilities, feel disempowered, and disengage. Instead of stepping up, they withdraw, stop trying, or give up entirely.

So, let's dive into what it really means to empower others to make decisions—and how mastering this practice can transform your team's effectiveness, trust, and culture.

The Art of Empowering People to Make Decisions

Empowering others to make decisions isn't just about handing off tasks—it's about building confidence, trust, and a sense of ownership. It's about creating an environment where people are encouraged to think for themselves, take initiative, and trust in their own judgment, without worrying they'll fail.

When you empower people to make decisions, you're showing that you value their perspective and trust their ability and approach to problem-solving. This kind of trust lights a fire; it sparks creativity, deepens responsibility, and inspires people to bring their best thinking forward. Empowered individuals don't just complete tasks—they innovate, lead, and care deeply about the success of the team.

Here is the key: when people feel trusted to make decisions, they become more confident. At the same time, their trust in you grows too—whether you're a leader, teammate, or partner. It creates a ripple effect: when people feel trusted, they take ownership, contributing with greater energy that brings their best ideas forward. In turn, outcomes improve, and people take pride in their contributions.

In all aspects of relationships—whether as a leader, a teammate, or even a parent—empowering others to make decisions begins with self-awareness. Sometimes, without meaning to, we can unintentionally become a bottleneck. We may fall into the trap of second-guessing, over-reviewing, or stepping in too soon. When that micromanagement happens, it blocks creativity and shuts down initiative. On the flip side, when we step back and trust, we create space for innovation, ownership, and real growth.

The art of empowering people to make decisions lies in striking the right balance. It's knowing when to offer support and when to let go, creating the space for others to succeed and confidently step into their authority.

Mastering the Art of Empowering People to Make Decisions

Mastering the art of empowering people to make decisions builds trust, fuels innovation, and brings teams closer together.

When people know their judgment is respected and valued, they become more resilient, creative, and committed. This trust lifts everyone, creating an environment where people and ideas can thrive.

Empowering others isn't accidental—it's a conscious choice that requires intentional practice. Here is how to put empowerment into practice with clarity and purpose:

Encourage ownership and independent decision-making. Help individuals know their decision-making authority, then trust them to act. Empowerment begins when people know their judgment is valued.

Support their growth, not just their success. Recognize past successes and reinforce people's ability to make sound decisions. Affirm that you stand behind them—and celebrate wins.

Create flexibility and space for innovation. Honor different approaches to success while staying available to support, guide, and uplift when needed.

Empowering people to make decisions unlocks their potential, strengthens trust, and fuels momentum. When you extend your trust in their ability to decide, you help them build trust in themselves.

Involve Others and Seek Their Input

Thomas was leading a high-stakes product launch that could shape the company's future. Instead of relying solely on his expertise, he brought his team in as true partners.

In a key strategy meeting, he asked, "What challenges do you see? What ideas do you have to make this launch a success?" Though hesitant at first, the team soon uncovered crucial insights: Daniela flagged a messaging gap that could have alienated customers, and Jorge spotted a logistical issue that could have delayed the launch.

Thanks to their insights, Thomas adjusted the plan and steered clear of those risks. When the launch succeeded, Thomas didn't take the spotlight—he stood before the team and said, "This success belongs to all of us."

The true win wasn't just a flawless product release—it was a team transformed: more confident, more committed, and more connected than ever.

By seeking input, Thomas did more than just make decisions. He built trust. He deepened relationships. And most importantly, he fostered a culture of shared ownership. When people feel heard, it activates a powerful chain reaction—engagement grows, collaboration deepens, and everyone is more likely to bring their best thinking to the table.

Think about a time when someone asked for your opinion. How did it feel? Empowering? Validating? Being invited to contribute is more than acknowledgment—it's a reminder that your voice matters.

Now, reflect on a time when you sought someone else's input. How did their insights help you? Perhaps they helped you see a challenge more clearly, uncover new options, or find a better path forward.

Every time we exchange ideas, we strengthen trust, deepen connection, and fuel creativity—the very foundation of lasting collaboration.

Now, let's explore the art of involving others and how mastering this practice can transform the quality of your relationships.

The Art of Involving Others and Seeking Their Input

The art of involving others is rooted in intentionality—a courageous choice to create a culture of trust, collaboration, and shared ownership. When you ask for someone's input, invite their perspective, or better yet, brainstorm together, you're sending a powerful message: their experience, creativity, and judgment matter. That's because the act of asking for input can have profound effects.

But here's the key: it must be authentic. Asking for input without true openness—what some would call "lip service"—can backfire. If people share their thoughts and feel ignored or dismissed, it chips away at trust. They might feel undervalued, disheartened, or disillusioned, disengaging over time. The next time you ask for their involvement, they may withdraw or offer only minimal effort, undermining the potential for meaningful collaboration and success.

True involvement requires reflection, compassion, and the willingness to act on what you hear—because inviting someone's perspective is not just an action; it's a relationship built on mutual respect and courage. In essence, involving others creates a virtuous cycle: *trust begets trust, and collaboration fosters growth.*

The true art of involvement requires genuine curiosity, openness, and respect for the contributions of others. Involving others and seeking their input is about more than solving a single problem; it cultivates a culture rich in trust, creativity, and mutual respect.

When you embrace diverse perspectives and encourage genuine collaboration, you unlock the full potential of your team and relationships. This practice not only improves results but also lays the groundwork for a more connected and productive future.

Mastering the Art of Involving Others and Seeking Their Input

Mastering the art of involving others starts with intention and is carried out with thoughtful, consistent actions that strengthen trust and collaboration. Based on our research and real-world experience, here's how you can do it well:

Clarify your intentions and stay open. Be clear about what you're aiming to achieve but stay open to new ideas and perspectives you didn't anticipate.

Invite and welcome diverse voices. Step outside your comfort zone to seek out different viewpoints with genuine curiosity. Listen fully—even when others' input challenges your assumptions.

Act on what you hear. Acknowledge others' input, show how it influenced the outcome, and stay transparent. Trust grows when people see that their voice matters.

Appreciate every contribution. Thank people sincerely for their ideas, effort, and courage. Gratitude strengthens connection and invites future collaboration.

Involving others isn't just a leadership skill—it's a life skill. Whether at work, at home, or in your community, seeking and valuing input builds trust, strengthens connection, and leads to better outcomes for everyone.

Help People Learn Skills

Mariana was a dedicated worker who often doubted her ability to lead, staying quiet in meetings. Her manager,

Felipe, saw her potential and encouraged her to lead an upcoming client presentation.

Though Mariana was hesitant, Felipe reassured her: "No one ever feels fully ready. But I believe in you—and I'll help you prepare." Over the next few weeks, he coached her through organizing key points and helped her practice presenting with confidence.

When the day came, Mariana delivered a poised, impressive presentation that opened new opportunities for the team. Afterward, Felipe simply said, "Growth often starts with someone believing in you—before you fully believe in yourself."

Have you ever considered how your belief in others enables them to believe in themselves?

When you encourage people to stretch beyond what they know, you don't just help them build new skills—you help them trust in their own abilities. Investing in someone's growth allows them to experience what they are truly capable of, often breaking through self-limiting beliefs they didn't even realize they carried.

Encouraging others to step outside their comfort zones is one of the most powerful ways to foster growth and lay the groundwork for lasting success. When people feel genuinely supported, their confidence soars. They become more adaptable, resilient, and able to face uncertainty—not with fear, but with energy, self-trust, and the knowledge that they have what it takes to grow and evolve.

Whether through mentorship, peer coaching, or creating opportunities for growth—you ignite potential. You shape a workplace that is brighter, stronger, more capable, and better prepared for the future.

The best part? Knowledge is a gift that lasts a lifetime. When you invest in others, you don't just impact their journey—you shape the success of their life, your team, your workplace, and your community.

The Art of Helping People Learn Skills

The art of helping others learn and grow goes beyond offering tools or resources—it's about showing trust in people's potential, recognizing them as whole individuals, and actively investing in their development. The impact runs deep. When you support someone's learning, you offer more than skills—you communicate a belief in their ability to rise to adapt and evolve into the best version of themselves.

This act of trust strengthens relationships, boosts individual and team performance, and nurtures cultures where confidence, resilience, and growth can flourish. Everyone benefits because someone chose to believe in them.

Helping others grow isn't just about building tangible expertise; it's about fostering qualities like empathy, communication, and adaptability. True learning shapes not just what we do, but who we become and how we bring our best selves to the people and communities around us.

Mastering the Art of Helping People Learn Skills

Mastering the art of helping others learn new skills begins with you—your willingness to encourage people, believe in them, and help them have the courage to trust their abilities. Growth isn't just the responsibility of formal training programs;

it's something we foster every day through small, intentional actions. Here's how:

Discover aspirations and strengths. Have open conversations about where people see themselves growing. Listen for their passions, strengths, and goals, and ask, *What skills or experiences would you love to build next?*

Create everyday opportunities to learn. Offer chances for growth—whether it's collaborating on a project; sharing resources like articles, books, or podcasts; or inviting someone to join you in new experiences. Learning is more powerful when it is shared.

Connect them to people and ideas. Help expand their network by introducing them to mentors, peers, or experts who can help guide their growth. Sometimes a single conversation or connection can open doors that change someone's path.

Lead by sharing your own growth story. Be open about your own learning journey, the challenges you faced, and how you keep moving forward. When you model vulnerability and perseverance, you inspire others to believe in their own potential.

Helping people learn new skills is one of the most powerful ways to invest in their future. It unlocks new possibilities for a more capable future—one that enriches relationships, teams, organizations, and the communities they serve.

Trust of Capability is built through everyday actions that recognize, empower, and elevate others. When you see people for who they are—and who they can become—you create the conditions for growth, collaboration, and shared success. Trust takes root when potential is believed in, nurtured, and given room to rise.

Looking Ahead

The Three Dimensions of Trust—Character, Communication, and Capability (figure 8)—form the core of how trust is built and sustained.[2] This model illustrates how each dimension contributes to our overall capacity for trust and how, together, they create a dynamic, reciprocal foundation for strong relationships.

We've now explored the Three Dimensions of Trust—each distinct, each essential. Trust of Character is built by showing genuine commitment to others' success. Trust of Communication comes alive through honest, open, and meaningful dialogue. Trust of Capability increases when we encourage learning, development, and growth.

While each dimension can be practiced on its own, trust is never one-dimensional. These three dimensions work in concert—strengthening and reinforcing one another with every choice we make. When practiced consistently, they form the foundation for relationships rooted in respect, collaboration, and

TRUST OF
CAPABILITY®

- Acknowledge people's skills and abilities
- Empower people to make decisions
- Involve others and seek their input
- Help people learn skills

TRUST OF
CHARACTER®

- Manage expectations
- Establish boundaries
- Delegate appropriately
- Encourage mutually serving intentions
- Keep agreements
- Be consistent

RECIPROCAL

CAPACITY FOR
TRUST®

CREATED INCREMENTALLY

TRUST OF
COMMUNICATION®

- Share information
- Tell the truth
- Admit mistakes
- Give and receive constructive feedback
- Maintain confidentiality
- Speak with good purpose

Figure 8. Reina Dimensions of Trust: The Three Cs

mutual empowerment. This is how trust is built. This is how it's sustained. And this is how it becomes a lasting force for connection, transformation, and shared success.

Change is inevitable—and with it comes moments of doubt, disruption, and the imperfections that make us human. As we've seen, trust is powerful, but it isn't indestructible. No one navigates this flawlessly. We will falter. Trust will be tested. Sometimes it weakens gradually through neglect or misalignment; other times, it's broken in a single moment.

To build relationships where trust can truly endure, we must also understand what weakens it—how it becomes fragile, and what causes it to break. This is the work of the next chapter: exploring the vulnerable, often unseen threads that hold trust together and what happens when they begin to unravel, break down, and erode.

CHAPTER FIVE

The Fragile Threads of Trust

Navigating Breaches and Betrayal

The trials you face will introduce you to your strengths.
EPICTETUS

Trust is the foundation of all meaningful relationships—and yet, it is inherently fragile. As human beings, we will inevitably face moments when trust is strained, eroded, or even broken—not because we are flawed or malicious, but because we are human. Disappointment and betrayal are not signs of failure; they are part of the complex, imperfect reality of being in relationship with others.

When we think of broken trust or betrayal, our minds often go to major offenses—things like lying, stealing, or deliberate manipulation. In business, it might look like withholding critical information during a high-stakes deal. In personal relationships, it could be hiding debt or maintaining a secret relationship. These behaviors clearly undermine the honesty and reliability that trust depends on.

You might be thinking, *I don't do those things*—and chances are, you don't. Most people don't. But here's the hard truth: trust is more often eroded by the small, subtle, and unintentional actions that slip into our everyday interactions—not the dramatic breaches, but the quiet ones we often overlook.

Our years of research have shown that 90 percent of behaviors that break trust in workplace relationships are minor, subtle, and unintentional, such as the ones you'll see in figure 9, the Betrayal Continuum.[1] Most of us both experience *and* contribute to these moments. It's rarely intentional. Very few people set out to disappoint, let down, overlook, or undermine others. Just as you likely don't intend to do that to anyone else. Yet, it happens. In the day-to-day complexities of work and human interaction, trust is constantly being tested—even in small ways we may not realize.

> *George misses another deadline. Heather shares difficult news and gets shut down. Mary rolls her eyes. Harry is gossiping about Jane. Tom cancels the meeting again—for the third time. Mark refuses to address "the situation." Then comes the meeting after the meeting. One department blames the other. Someone claims credit for work they didn't do. You find yourself chasing down the same deliverable, again and again.*

THE BETRAYAL CONTINUUM

MINOR		MAJOR	
UNINTENTIONAL	**INTENTIONAL**	**UNINTENTIONAL**	**INTENTIONAL**
• Repeatedly late to work	• Gossiping; backbiting	• Restructuring; layoffs	• Disclosing proprietary information
• Not keeping agreements	• Accepting credit for others' work	• Delegating without giving authority	• Actively disengaged; disrupting systems

Figure 9: The Betrayal Continuum

Sound familiar?

When trust is broken—*whether by others or by yourself*—it can leave behind lingering feelings of confusion, pain, and self-doubt. These moments shake our sense of security, challenge our self-worth, and disrupt our connection to the people and the world around us.

In the aftermath, it's easy to fall into the trap of resentment, replaying the hurt, brooding over the injustice, and imagining how things should have gone. Pain can consume our focus, erode our sense of peace, cause us to want to seek justice, and fuel a cycle of anger and self-pity. Over time, we may begin to show up in ways that feel distant, guarded, or even bitter to those around us.

The first step toward healing is gaining a deeper understanding of what caused the breach—because with awareness comes the power to choose a different path forward.

In this chapter, you will explore the vulnerability of trust. You will deepen your awareness and be empowered to make more conscious choices regarding how you show up and behave:

- Embracing vulnerability

- Expanding your trust perspective

- Building confidence when trust is broken

Acknowledging betrayal—whether major or minor, intentional or unintentional—begins with awareness and compassion. By embracing both, you create the space to face betrayal with courage and honesty. Choosing to confront your pain, rather than avoid it, allows you to reclaim your sense of wholeness and step into deeper personal strength. And when you embrace the vulnerability that trust requires, you open yourself to more authentic and meaningful connections. Vulnerability, once seen as a risk, becomes the pathway to true healing, connection, and lasting trust.

As Dennis has said countless times throughout our lives together, *I am grateful for my experiences of betrayal because of how they contributed to the person I am today. They led me to the relationships I hold most precious, and to where I am in my life.*

Embracing Vulnerability

Giving yourself permission to be vulnerable is not a weakness, as is often perceived—it's a profound strength. When trust is broken—*whether you have been betrayed, have betrayed someone else, or want to support others through betrayal*—there is always an opportunity for growth.

Just as ecosystems are interconnected systems of nature, relationships are interconnected systems of humanity. That's why it is rare for someone to fit neatly into just one category or role. Often, we occupy multiple roles at once—hurt and hurting, betrayed and betrayer, protector and participant. If someone has broken your trust, honest self-reflection may reveal ways you've also contributed to the breakdown—or how your actions may stem from a reaction to being betrayed yourself.

Unbeknownst to coworkers and teammates, often people engage in trust breaking behavior at work because of personal betrayals at home.

This unconscious, cyclical nature of betrayal reinforces the importance of understanding and breaking the negative pattern. Only through understanding can we begin to break the pattern—and choose a different way forward.

Mia sat in the conference room, staring at the slides projected on the screen. Every chart, every insight, every late-night hour behind them was hers. Yet it was Jeremy, her colleague, standing at the front of the room, presenting the work as if it were his own.

A tightness gripped Mia's chest. She had trusted him and shared her drafts openly, believing they were collaborating. Now, she watched as he claimed the credit, leaving her stunned by the betrayal.

Moments like these reveal just how vulnerable trust really is.

To fully know trust—and to embrace it and live it—we must also understand its fragility. Knowing what breaks trust or causes it to collapse helps us to build, honor, and sustain it. Whether emotional or psychological, true appreciation of vulnerability comes from experiencing hurt, disappointment, or judgment. This is why vulnerability is not a weakness.

Instead, it's about letting down your guard and showing up as your full, authentic self—complete with imperfections, flaws, and uncertainties. It means embracing your fears and insecurities, even when you've been pushed outside your comfort zone. Especially in the wake of betrayal, whether admitting mistakes or daring to rebuild trust—vulnerability takes courage, and it starts with self-trust.

Embracing vulnerability within ourselves is just the beginning. In any workplace, whether you're leading a team, collaborating with peers, or supporting others through challenges, your willingness to show up with openness sets the tone. Vulnerability, when practiced with intention, becomes a powerful invitation—one that helps others lower their guard, speak their truth, and step into trust alongside you.

The greatest barrier to embracing vulnerability is fear—fear of rejection, fear of judgment, and fear of appearing weak.

Overcoming this fear begins with small, intentional steps, such as admitting a mistake at work, asking for help, or sharing a personal story with a trusted colleague. Because trust is a reciprocal force, leaders have a powerful role to play. By being transparent about challenges—like organizational shifts, mergers, or workforce reductions—they model courage and honesty, which deepens trust and strengthens connections.

For a trustworthy leader, fostering a culture of trust starts with showing vulnerability—living out the principles and behaviors presented in the Three Dimensions of Trust. Showing your "warts and flaws" does not make you weak. It makes you relatable, humble, human, and ultimately trustworthy.

As you reflect on your role as a trusted leader or a team member others can turn to, use this moment to pause and reflect on a few important questions:

- *Am I honoring the dignity of every person I encounter— without judgment, bias, or favoritism?*

- *Do I stand for the dignity of others, even when it's inconvenient or uncomfortable?*

- *Am I seeing and honoring the humanity in everyone I lead, without letting assumptions cloud my view?*

Trust is not built in a single moment. It's earned through the consistency of your attitude, your mindset, and your actions. Trust begins with you—and the courage to grow in your self-awareness. As you learn to trust in yourself, expand your willingness to trust others, and live the behaviors of the Three Dimensions of Trust, you'll begin to see the difference: walls come down, and meaningful connection takes root.

No matter where you sit in life, you lead through your choices, actions, and presence. Whether in a formal role or working alongside others, your honesty, authenticity, and vulnerability give others permission to show the same. When people feel safe to express concerns or uncertainties, they develop confidence, resilience, and problem-solving abilities. If they always look to you for answers, they miss the chance to build their own.

Simply saying, *I don't know yet*, can open the door to collaboration, creativity, and shared learning. When you embrace vulnerability—both in yourself and with others—you create space for healing, growth, and relationships built on trust and authenticity.

Expanding Your Trust Perspective

Trust is vulnerable by nature—and that vulnerability shows up in different ways depending on your experience. At times, you are the one who unintentionally hurt or disappoint others. Other times, you're on the receiving end—left navigating the pain of broken trust. And often, you find yourself in a third role: supporting someone else through their own experience of betrayal.

In the sections that follow, you'll explore key guidance for navigating each of these moments with awareness, accountability, and care. These vantage points help us understand how the vulnerability of trust presents itself:

- At some point in life, you will find yourself hurt, disappointed, or let down by others.

- Whether intentional or not on your part, others are going to feel hurt, disappointed, or let down by you.

- At other times, you'll be called to support someone whose trust has been broken.

Each vantage point offers a valuable opportunity for expanding your perspective and growing through the process. Whether you're the one who caused the hurt, the one who was hurt, or the one offering support, your perspective holds insight—and the potential to rebuild connection, deepen compassion, and strengthen trust.

Trust's fragility offers valuable opportunities for growth, no matter which perspective you find yourself in. In the sections that follow, you'll find insights to guide you through each experience.

Understanding the Interconnectedness of Relationships

Trust doesn't exist in isolation. Human relationships are part of a larger, interconnected system. When trust is broken, honest reflection can reveal how you may have contributed to the breakdown—through actions, inaction, or reactions shaped by past experiences.

Often, the harm we cause isn't rooted in the present moment, but in unresolved pain carried from one relationship to another. In this way, betrayal can become cyclical, repeating itself across both personal and professional spaces.

Recognizing this pattern offers a powerful opportunity: to break the cycle rather than continue it. By choosing self-awareness, accountability, and compassion, you begin to create new, healthier patterns of trust—where healing becomes possible and connection can be restored.

Nathan knew the moment he hit "send" that he had made a mistake. His friend and coworker, Elise, had confided in him about her struggles balancing work and caring for her sick mother. It wasn't meant to be public knowledge. But in a moment of frustration, when their manager questioned Elise's recent absences, Nathan blurted out the truth.

Later, when he saw Elise's teary eyes in the break room, guilt hit him hard. He hadn't meant to betray her trust, but his intent didn't erase the impact. When he finally apologized, Elise's quiet but firm response cut deep: "You didn't think about how this would affect me? Now everyone looks at me with pity instead of respect."

From that moment, Nathan vowed to do better. He became fiercely protective of others' trust, learning that sometimes silence is the strongest form of loyalty.

The Prevalence of Broken Trust in the Workplace

Broken trust is common in many environments, especially workplaces. Even if you are not directly involved, you can feel its presence. When trust is compromised, energy contracts. People withdraw. You may not know the details of what happened, but you know something is off.

When friends or colleagues are hurting, it's natural to want to help. Many well-meaning people ask how they can support others in rebuilding trust. But before reaching out, it's essential to reflect on your own relationship to betrayal. Why? Because helping others navigate their trust issues can trigger emotions tied to your own unresolved experiences, whether from work, personal relationships, or even early life. To truly be a source of strength, start by tending to your own healing. People are more likely to trust and open up to someone who is not only empathetic but also grounded—someone who has done the inner work and leads with authenticity and emotional clarity.

*David felt a familiar sting as he watched his supervisor dis-
miss Rachel's work in front of the team. The way she sat in
stunned silence, hurt flickering in her eyes, reminded him
of times when his own voice had been ignored. The urge to
react surged—but he caught himself. This moment wasn't
about him.*

*Later in the break room, he approached her. "That wasn't
fair," he said. "Your work was solid. If you want, I'll back you
up when you talk with him."*

*Rachel hesitated, but David's steady presence gave her
just enough courage to speak up. That afternoon, she confronted their supervisor, standing up for her contributions
while David stood by. It wasn't easy, but it was a step toward
reclaiming her confidence.*

In that moment, David understood something deeper:
trust isn't only about stepping in—it's about standing with. It's
about creating the safety and support others need to find their
own voice.

The (Subtle Yet Significant) Impact of
Trust Breaking Behaviors

We've uncovered an important truth: most breaches of trust don't
happen through dramatic betrayal—they happen through small,
often unintentional acts. On their own, these moments may seem
too minor to matter. You may offer grace, dismiss them, or simply
look the other way. Yet their quiet accumulation carries a cost too
great to ignore.

As you read these everyday examples, notice which ones feel
familiar to you—either from your own experience or from your

own behavior. These are ordinary moments where trust begins to fray:

Gossiping behind backs: You share something in confidence, and it becomes office gossip. Trust disappears instantly.

Blaming the messenger: Someone speaks up about an issue but gets criticized instead of being heard. Honesty gets shut down.

Taking credit for others' work: You do the heavy lifting, but someone else claims the praise. Over time, you stop speaking up.

Saying one thing; doing another: Leaders talk about accountability but miss deadlines. Colleagues preach teamwork but don't follow through. Actions don't match words.

Overlooking effort: You work hard and go the extra mile, but it's ignored or brushed aside. Motivation fades.

Breaking confidentiality: You confide in someone, only to hear your words repeated elsewhere. You pull back from trusting again.

Being inconsistent: One day supportive, the next distant or critical. The unpredictability makes trust impossible.

Holding grudges: A disagreement turns into the cold shoulder, sarcasm, or subtle revenge. Conflict deepens instead of healing.

Micromanaging: Every move you make is second-guessed. You feel controlled, not trusted.

Dodging responsibility: Mistakes happen, but instead of owning them, people make excuses and shift blame. Others are left to clean up.

All too often, we normalize these behaviors. We shrug them off as *just how things are around here.* But, in that resignation, we lose sight of how deeply they affect us—and those around us.

Minor breaches, when accumulated over time, can have an impact just as profound as major betrayal. Anger, resentment, and disappointment creep in. Confidence wavers. Pride in our work dims; motivation fades. People pull back—not out of spite but out of self-protection. And, with each withdrawal, the energy of trust contracts further, creating a cycle that becomes harder to reverse.

But awareness is powerful. The more clearly we see these patterns, the more choice we have in how we respond. Every insight brings you one step closer to healthier, more trusting connections—within yourself and with others.

Turning the Mirror: Recognizing Your Role in Trust Dynamics

It's easy to notice when someone else breaks trust—but have you ever considered your own role in the equation? Trust isn't just something that happens to us; it's something you actively build or weaken through your own behavior, whether intentional or not. That's why, again and again, we emphasize that trust begins with you—and requires your willingness to grow in awareness.

Take a moment to reflect: Have you ever dismissed someone's ideas too quickly? Been inconsistent in your actions? Shared someone's work or insights without giving them full recognition? Interrupted someone without truly listening? Failed to follow through on a promise, even if unintentionally? Maybe you didn't mean to, but even small actions can erode trust over time.

This isn't about blame—it's about *awareness.* When you pause and honestly assess your role in these dynamics, you gain the power to shift your awareness.

Where might you be contributing—directly or indirectly—to a breakdown of trust in your relationships, whether at work or at home? More importantly, what small changes could you make to rebuild and strengthen trust?

Building Confidence When Trust Is Shaken

Let's face it: the unraveling of trust or betrayal is one of the most difficult experiences to navigate. When your trust is betrayed, it leaves you questioning not only the motives of others but also your own ability to trust again. You find yourself wondering where you belong and questioning your own value and worth.

Yet as painful as betrayal can be, it also holds the potential for profound growth. If we allow it, it can become both a teacher and a turning point. It urges us to explore why we—and others—get stuck in cycles of mistrust, while also illuminating unmet needs and pointing us toward healing. At its core, betrayal acts as a mirror, reflecting the fragile and complex nature of human connection.

Rebuilding trust, both in yourself and in others, requires rebuilding confidence. Imagine a moment of betrayal—a trusted colleague taking credit for your work or a loved one breaking a promise. The pain can be sharp and feel overwhelming. It's natural to want to pull away or shut down, even to become paralyzed. But what if, *instead of retreating from the discomfort, you paused long enough to feel it?* What if you allowed yourself to sit with the pain, understand its source, and from there begin to chart a new path forward?

To take this one step further, imagine you're on the other side of a betrayal, whole and healed. The storm has passed, and you've weathered it with resilience, courage, and fortitude. You've even taken steps to rebuild trust—first in yourself, then in others.

Along the way, you've faced fears and stepped beyond familiar limits. Maybe the worst didn't happen. Maybe, by extending trust in small, deliberate ways, you not only repaired a relationship but also discovered a deeper strength within yourself. Each choice to trust—even when it felt risky—helped rebuild your confidence and expanded your capacity for connection.

This journey takes practice. It takes courage to face discomfort and compassion to stay with it. Sometimes it begins with something as simple as giving a colleague the benefit of the doubt or sharing a personal story with someone you've hesitated to open up to. And yet each time you choose to extend trust, you push past your comfort zone. With every moment of vulnerability, you grow stronger.

Rebuilding trust may feel daunting, but it *is* essential. Because trust is rarely shattered by one dramatic moment. More often, it fades bit by bit through small disappointments—missed acknowledgments, unspoken frustrations, and quiet inconsistencies. Over time, these tiny cracks add up, widening the gap. But just as trust can fade gradually, it can also be restored—through steady, intentional choices, one moment at a time.

When trust is damaged, it often affects more than just the individuals involved. In workplaces, especially, broken trust can spread like wildfire, creating undercurrents of suspicion, disengagement, and fear. You may have seen it firsthand: a team member quietly gossiping behind someone's back, or a leader who consistently overlooks contributions. These seemingly minor behaviors send subtle but powerful signals, weakening the culture from the inside out.

Rebuilding trust in these environments begins with one essential step: introspection. Ask yourself, *Am I showing up as someone others can trust? Do my words and actions align?*

From there, the work becomes relational: rebuilding connection, encouraging honest dialogues, fostering spaces where people feel safe to be open and real.

As you navigate the delicate process of rebuilding trust, remember this: *every setback, every disappointment, and every moment of vulnerability is also a moment of possibility.* Trust may be fragile, but it is equally resilient. With patience, reflection, self-awareness, and a sincere effort to make wrongs right, trust can be rebuilt—stronger, wiser, and more grounded than before.

The vulnerability of trust can lead to pain—but it can also be a powerful catalyst for growth. In the next chapter, you'll explore how pain, when acknowledged and processed, becomes a stepping stone to healing—and how broken trust, when tended to with care, can lead to renewal.

The bottom line is this: when you choose to trust, you plant seeds of hope—both for the present and for what's possible in the future.

CHAPTER SIX

Rebuilding Trust

A Pathway to Healing

Healing takes courage, and we all have courage,
even if we must dig a little to find it.
TORI AMOS

We do not live in isolation. We are woven into the fabric of humanity and shaped by the relationships that accompany us through life. These connections—fragile, dynamic, yet deeply meaningful—are among the most precious elements of our existence. The relationships that endure are grounded in trust. But that doesn't mean they are free from pain. Even the strongest bonds can be touched by hurt, disappointment, or betrayal.

As we explored in the previous chapter, when trust is broken, it leaves a lasting emotional imprint. You've felt it: the silent tension in a once close relationship . . . the friend who faded away without explanation . . . the family member who no longer speaks your name . . . the aunt who was once a cherished part of your childhood but has slowly faded from your life . . . the sibling who no longer returns your calls . . . the partner who, despite your deep connection, was never fully welcomed into your extended family.

These are not abstract examples. You know them; you have lived them. Some you may still carry with you today.

These aren't just relational shifts—they are quiet reminders of how trust, once broken, can create a distance that words alone often cannot mend. **When trust is eroded, lost, or betrayed, it leaves a profound emotional imprint that can linger for years.**

Broken trust creates inner fractures that don't just disappear with time. They call for acknowledgment. They invite reflection. And eventually, they demand healing—if we are to stay healthy and whole, we must grow forward with the relationships that matter.

When trust is shattered, you are faced with a pivotal choice:

- *Remain in pain as a victim.*

- *Take courageous steps forward to confront and heal the wounds.*

The truth is no one walks through life without pain or struggle. What defines our path isn't the absence of pain but how we choose to respond to it. Do we close ourselves off, or do we meet the moment with honesty, resilience, and hope? Difficulties are inevitable, but they don't have to block our way. With intention, they can become stepping stones for growth—guiding us toward deeper understanding and stronger intention.

There's a story about the young Michael Caine, early in his acting career. While rehearsing a scene for the movie *Alfie* (1966), he was blocked by a chair jammed in a doorway. His first instinct was to stop and declare the scene unworkable. But the partner in the scene encouraged him to "use the challenge to your advantage." If the scene was a comedy, trip over it. If it was a drama, knock it down.[1]

Caine attributes that as a defining moment shaping his approach to life: use what's in front of you, adapt, and move forward.

The same applies when trust is broken. You can't always change what happened. But you can choose how you respond. You can use the pain as a teacher, a catalyst for growth. You can turn the fracture into a doorway that becomes a defining moment.

Rebuilding trust—within yourself and with others—isn't easy. It takes courage, compassion, and a willingness to grow. But you don't have to do it alone. Let's walk this path together.

In the pages ahead, you'll explore how trust can be rebuilt—not all at once, but through intentional steps that invite healing, growth, and clarity. You'll examine this journey through

- The Seven Steps for Healing

- The role of forgiveness

- Navigating change using the Seven Steps

Whether you're feeling the sting of betrayal, coming to terms with having hurt someone else, or walking alongside someone in their healing, the journey back to trust takes more than time—it takes intention and a genuine willingness to grow.

The Seven Steps for Healing are here to guide you.[2] They offer a clear, compassionate path for making sense of the pain, repairing what's been broken, and opening the door to something even more powerful: transformation. As you move through this process, you'll find that rebuilding trust isn't just possible—it's a vital part of reclaiming your strength, clarity, and connection. And along the way, you may just uncover deeper truths about who you are.

The Seven Steps for Healing

The *Seven Steps for Healing* model offers a universal lens to help people step into and move through the pain that comes with broken trust. Rooted in both research and lived experience, this model has evolved through our work with hundreds of organizations around the world—and just as importantly, through our own personal journeys.

This framework was born from Dennis's deeply personal experience navigating the pain of betrayal. In the wake of dishonesty, broken promises, and abandonment during a painful divorce, Dennis realized that healing wasn't simply about moving on. It was about making sense of what had happened, understanding the deeper lessons, and finding a way to forgive—not only the other person, but himself. Through this journey, he learned to release the pain and reclaim his strength. The model that emerged from that experience—shaped by reflection and reinforced through years of research and experience—became the *Seven Steps for Healing*.

The Seven Steps for Healing offer a clear and compassionate, structured path for learning to trust again—even after deep hurt. Informed by extensive research on grief, this model recognizes that betrayal often feels like a kind of death. It brings a profound sense of loss and a whirlwind of emotions: shock, anger, denial, and eventually acceptance. Much like grief, healing from broken trust requires us to move through these feelings, gradually making room for understanding and what the future can hold.

The Seven Steps for Healing model (see figure 10) provides practical guidance. It helps you identify what happened, process the pain, and begin to move forward with clarity. As you engage with each step, you'll be invited to reflect, take ownership, explore forgiveness, and begin to let go—at your own pace. In doing so, betrayal becomes more than just a wound; it becomes a teacher—offering insight not just into your relationships, but into yourself.

This framework supports you in understanding what happened, processing the pain, and finding a clearer path forward. As you move through each step, you'll be encouraged to take responsibility, seek or offer forgiveness, and begin to let go. In doing so, betrayal can become a powerful teacher—offering insight not just into your relationships, but into yourself and into life.

Ultimately, these steps are here to provide both emotional insight and practical tools to help you heal and rebuild.

While the Seven Steps are presented in a sequence, each person's journey is unique and nonlinear—full of pauses, reflections, and leaps.

Each of the Seven Steps represents distinct aspects of the healing process. Although they are numbered for clarity, healing does not always happen in a straight line. It's common to move between steps, experience several at once, or revisit certain steps

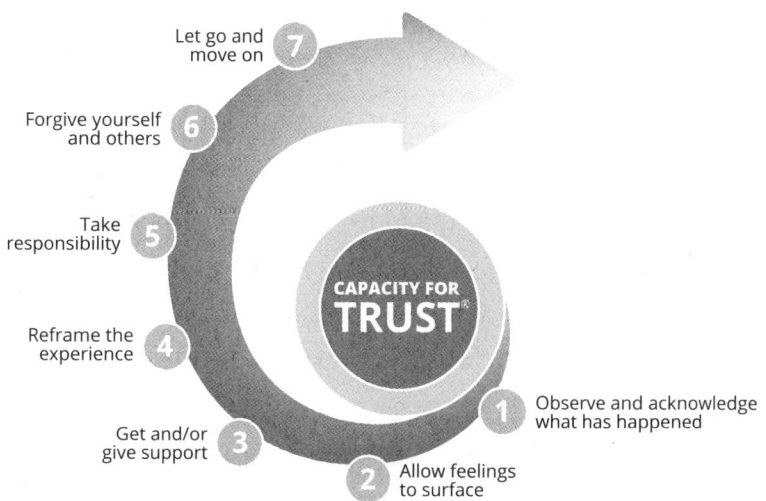

Figure 10. Seven Steps for Healing

depending on the situation and your emotional readiness. For instance, you might begin by acknowledging what happened (step 1) while also starting to process your emotions and feelings (step 2). Reaching out for support (step 3) can also happen early and play a pivotal role. No matter where you begin, healing always starts with facing the truth of what's happened—and from there, it unfolds in a way that is unique to you.

Healing often moves like the tides and comes in waves—full of crests, troughs, and unpredictable currents. It's normal to feel like you're taking one step forward and two steps back. Even when progress feels slow or uneven, engaging with the Seven Steps keeps you moving toward growth.

At the core of this journey is self-compassion. Healing starts from within and calls for deep introspection, reflection, and intentional self-care. Prioritizing your well-being isn't a sign of weakness—it's a vital part of building resilience, strength, and renewal.

The Seven Steps provide the structure, but it's your courage and commitment to the process that unlocks true healing. Let's now walk through the Seven Steps—both the defining structure of the steps and supporting prompts and considerations you can use while moving through the journey:

Step 1: Observe and acknowledge what happened. Healing begins with truth—acknowledging what happened and the impact on you. Acknowledge not just the event itself, but the pain, the loss, and how it changed you, your relationships, and perhaps even the future you once imagined. Maybe it cost you an opportunity, a sense of safety, or a vision you held.

- *What happened?*

- *What is most important for me to acknowledge?*

- *What was the impact of this experience on me and my relationship?*

Step 2: Allow feelings to surface. Tune into your feelings—they are speaking to you and deserve your attention. Emotions are not obstacles to healing; they are stepping stones toward it. When you bottle them up or push them aside, you only slow your own path to wholeness. Whether you are feeling anger, sadness, confusion, or grief, give yourself permission to feel it all. Let the tears come. Write your thoughts down. Every time you honor what you feel, you open the door a little wider to healing.

- *What emotions am I experiencing? What emotions am I feeling right now?*

- *How can I verbalize my pain? How can I express my pain in a way that supports me?*

- *What safe ways can I practice releasing my feelings?*

Step 3: Get support. You don't have to do this alone. Healing happens faster and deeper with support, whether from a friend, therapist, or coach, or even through self-reflection. Support helps you shift from blame to problem-solving, allowing you to take responsibility for your growth.

- *What support do I need?*

- *Who in my life can I turn to for support?*

- *How can I reach out for the help I need?*

Step 4: Reframe the experience. Find meaning in the pain. Step back and look at the bigger picture. *What can this situation teach me? How can this experience shape my growth?* Consider extenuating circumstances that may be at play. Reframing allows you to find meaning in the struggle that comes with betrayal.

- *What is the bigger picture?*

- *What can I learn about myself or others?*

- *What new opportunities does this experience create for me?*

Step 5: Take responsibility. You cannot change what happened, but you can choose how you respond. While you may not be responsible for what happened, you are responsible for how you respond. Taking ownership means owning what you can do differently moving forward. Perhaps that means setting boundaries, communicating more openly, or offering an apology if needed.

- *What part of this situation is within my control?*

- *What actions can I take to grow from this?*

- *What promises do I need to make to myself and others?*

Step 6: Forgive yourself and others. Forgiveness is essential to healing. It's not about excusing what happened but about freeing yourself from the weight of anger, resentment, and pain. Forgiveness isn't about forgetting—it's about liberating yourself to move forward without being held hostage by your past.

- *What needs to happen for me to truly forgive?*

- *How does holding on to pain impact my well-being?*

- *How can forgiveness free me to live fully again?*

Step 7: Let go and move on. Letting go and moving on doesn't erase the past—it honors the past while you choose to move beyond it. Rather than dwelling on the betrayal, you focus on moving forward with purpose and clarity. By carrying the lessons and releasing the pain, you're able to step boldly into the life you are meant to live.

- *What steps can I take to leave this experience behind me?*

- *Have I given myself the time and space I need to process, heal, and commit to moving forward?*

- *How can I use this experience to shape a better future for myself?*

Healing is not about forgetting—it's about growing beyond what hurt you. It's a process, not a quick fix, and it takes time, patience, and intention. Broken trust does not mend itself; it requires your effort and commitment to work through the pain. The truth is, we've all stood on both sides—we've been hurt, and we have hurt others. Yet, at our core, most of us share the same instinct: to connect, to heal, and to do better.

No matter where you are on your healing journey, the Seven Steps for Healing are here to guide you. We designed them to help you work through your pain of betrayal, rebuild trust, and reconnect with your strength, confidence, and energy. So, take a moment to reflect: *How can I use these Seven Steps to move through feelings of hurt, disappointment, and broken trust and start moving forward with clarity and renewed conviction?*

Dennis's Journey: The Seven Steps in Action

As you may have observed throughout this book, the *art of trust building* serves all facets of our lives—those we work with, those we share time with, and those we live with and love. Understanding trust-related experiences in our personal lives can give us insight into the relationships in our professional lives and vice versa.

Dennis's journey through betrayal and healing is a story of how the Seven Steps can guide you from pain to renewal. Let's walk through his story and see how each step played a role in rebuilding trust, reclaiming his sense of self, and creating the life he leads today.

Step 1: Observe and acknowledge what happened. *Dennis's healing began when he confronted the painful truth that his focus on academic pursuits and parenting responsibilities distanced him from his wife, leaving him blindsided when he discovered her six-month affair with a coworker. Acknowledging this harsh truth was his first step toward rebuilding his life.*

Step 2: Allow feelings to surface. *Rather than suppressing his emotions, he met them head-on. He processed his feelings through physical activity, pounding out his frustrations during long runs through the woods and allowing the weight of his pain to fuel intense training in the gym, and he eventually found solace in raw, honest conversations in his men's group. He gave himself the opportunity to feel the depth of what was lost and to tune in to what that meant for his life.*

Step 3: Get support. *Realizing he could not do it alone, Dennis reached out for support. He turned to journaling, leaned on the brotherhood of his men's group, and stayed committed to weekly counseling with a therapist. He journaled his reflections—each insight helped him to work through his grief of losing his marriage and the family and life he once envisioned.*

Step 4: Reframe the experience. *Through deep self-exploration, Dennis shifted his perspective. Rather than seeing his divorce as the end of his life, he reframed it as a transition from one phase of life to the next. He took inventory of what he still had and what was most important to him—his boys. He began to envision a new way of life and see opportunities the future could hold. He continued to give himself room and space to process his feelings, using them as stepping stones for discovering a stronger, wiser version of himself.*

Step 5: Take responsibility. *One might say that Dennis had every reason to focus on the betrayal that occurred; however, he instead took an honest look at himself and recognized that his intense focus on earning his doctorate had created emotional distance in his marriage. Instead of dwelling on regret, he used this awareness as a turning point—committing not only to being more present in future relationships but also to deepening his connection with his sons, ensuring they always felt seen, valued, and loved.*

Step 6: Forgive yourself and others. *Dennis chose to offer compassion to himself, acknowledging his own missteps without harsh self-judgment. Through deep reflection, he recognized that holding onto guilt and beating himself up wouldn't change the past, but forgiving himself could shape his future. With that same grace, he extended forgiveness to his former spouse—not to excuse the betrayal and pain she caused, but to release the weight of resentment that had been holding him back. In letting go, he made room for healing, renewal, and peace.*

Step 7: Let go and move on. *Dennis's journey of healing wasn't about forgetting the past but about reclaiming himself, realigning with his values, and rebuilding trust—starting with himself. The* *loss of his marriage and the life he had envisioned with his sons deepened his understanding of trust's sacred nature. He realized that trust isn't automatic; it must be nurtured, protected, and continually renewed. This insight became a turning point, leading him to commit to lifelong growth, deeper self-awareness, and more intentional relationships.*

With new clarity, Dennis dedicated his doctoral research to exploring the complexities of trust building and its essential role in human connection. His path eventually led him to Michelle, a kindred spirit who shared his passion for relationships and personal growth. Together, we formed a partnership rooted in mutual trust and a shared mission to understand trust's profound impact on every part of life.

Driven by our emerging shared purpose, we entered the world of research and consulting, uncovering just how fragile—and rebuildable—trust can be. We realized that trust is not only the foundation of personal relationships but also the lifeblood of workplaces, teams, and organizations.

This insight ignited our life's work: helping individuals, teams, and organizations heal, strengthen, and renew trust. In 1999, we brought our mission to life with the first publication of *Trust and Betrayal in the Workplace*. More than a book, it became a road map for restoring broken trust. Our research continued to grow through two additional editions and later *Rebuilding Trust in the Workplace*, a deeper exploration of how to repair trust and cultivate cultures where it can truly thrive.

What began as Dennis's personal journey of healing became a body of work that has touched thousands. His pain opened new doors, deepened his purpose, and ultimately became a gift—a guide to help others rediscover connection, renewal, and lasting trust.

By becoming more fully aware of who you are, you expand your Capacity to Trust yourself and others. This journey isn't about changing who you are—it's about honoring and deepening the truth of who you have always been.

The Art of Letting Go and Moving Forward

Sometimes in the healing process, you get stuck. Holding on to pain can feel like carrying a weight that grows heavier over time. Letting go doesn't mean forgetting or dismissing what happened—it means choosing to free yourself so you can move forward with strength, clarity, and purpose. These reflections helped Dennis find his way through, and we hope they offer the same light for you.

What do you need to release to move on? Are there thoughts, feelings, or beliefs keeping you stuck? Acknowledge them, then ask yourself what it would take to let them go.

What needs to be said or done to bring closure? Is there something you need to say, do, or decide that would help you put this behind you?

What have you learned about yourself and relationships? Every challenge brings insight. What has this experience taught you about who you are, what matters to you, and how you want to show up?

What's one step you can take today? Healing happens little by little. Even the smallest action can begin to move you toward peace and renewal.

You don't have to rush your healing—but you do deserve peace. Trust that when the time is right, you'll know how to take the next brave step forward. And when you do, you'll be choosing yourself, your strength, and your future.

The Role of Forgiveness

Forgiveness? No way!

That's the reaction we often get in keynotes and workshops when we bring up forgiveness as part of rebuilding trust. People look at us like we're absurd. *There's no way I'm forgiving them*, they say. And honestly, we get it. When you've been hurt, betrayed, or let down, forgiveness can feel like the last thing you want to do.

But forgiveness is a cornerstone of healing. It can either propel you forward or keep you stuck. That's why we're giving it special attention here. Forgiveness isn't about forgetting or excusing what happened, or pretending the pain doesn't matter. It's about freeing yourself from the burden of resentment and anger. Holding on keeps you trapped in the past; letting go allows you to move forward with greater awareness, more resilience, and stronger boundaries.

When you forgive, you reclaim your energy. You clear space for what truly matters—building meaningful relationships, pursuing your goals, and growing into the person you are meant to be. Without forgiveness, pain lingers, quietly draining your spirit and limiting your progress.

Forgiveness isn't easy, and it doesn't happen overnight. It's a process—one that takes time, reflection, and grace. But whether you're rebuilding trust with others or with yourself, forgiveness is a powerful act of freedom.

Give yourself permission to heal at your own pace, knowing that each step opens the door to greater peace.

While trust can be broken, there are powerful steps you can take to release the weight of past betrayals, reclaim your strength, and rebuild trust in yourself and your relationships. Consider the following ways to reframe—in thought and action—so that forgiveness turns pain into strength:

Belief in irreparable damage → Reclaiming your future

Betrayal may have disrupted your path, but it doesn't have to shape your future. Forgiveness isn't about forgetting—it's about choosing to move forward on your own terms. You still have the power to create a life that's meaningful and yours.

Reframe: *This experience changed my path, but it doesn't define me. I can still create a meaningful and fulfilling life on my terms.*

Write down one small step you can take today to move forward—set a new goal, take one action toward a dream, or make a choice that reflects who you are becoming.

Waiting for atonement → Choosing your own closure

Waiting for an apology gives someone else power over your healing. True closure comes from within. You don't need their words to move forward—you can give yourself that freedom.

Reframe: *I don't need their apology to heal. I choose closure for myself.*

Write a letter to the person who hurt you—but don't send it. Say everything you need to say. Then release it in a way that feels right—tear it up, burn it, or tuck it away. Let this be your moment of closure.

Self-protection → Strength in boundaries

Forgiveness doesn't mean exposing yourself to more harm. In fact, it strengthens you. It helps you set clear boundaries, learn from past experiences, and trust yourself to recognize what is and isn't safe for your emotional well-being.

Reframe: *Forgiveness is strength. I can protect my heart and still choose to heal.*

Name one boundary you need to set or strengthen—whether it's limiting contact, speaking up for yourself, or deciding what you will no longer accept. Write it down and plan to act on it. This is how you protect your peace.

Humiliation or deceit → Restoring your own dignity

Betrayal can leave you feeling small—but forgiveness is how you stand tall again. It's a powerful way to say *I won't be defined by what was done to me.* Letting go of resentment frees you to move forward with self-respect.

Reframe: *I define my worth—not what happened to me. I choose dignity and strength.*

Do one thing today that affirms your value. Speak up, set a boundary, or simply remind yourself of the strength you carry. Each act of self-respect helps you rise and reclaim your power.

Lost opportunities → Embracing new possibilities

Yes, betrayal can close doors, but it can also open new ones. Forgiveness shifts your focus from what was lost to what is still possible. When you stop carrying the weight of resentment, you make space for new opportunities, experiences, and relationships to take shape.

Reframe: *The past is behind me, but my future is full of possibilities. I choose to move forward with hope.*

Name one new opportunity or experience you'd like to explore. It could be something small that excites you or that simply feels right. Then take one step—however small—toward it today. Make room for what's next.

Violated trust → Rebuilding trust in yourself

Betrayal shakes your faith in others—and in yourself. But forgiveness begins with restoring your own trust: in your instincts, your strengths, and your ability to move forward. It's not about trusting the one who hurt you—it's about trusting yourself again.

Reframe: *I may not trust them, but I trust myself. I have the strength and wisdom to move forward.*

Recall a time you listened to your intuition and made a good choice. Let that memory remind you of your inner wisdom. Today, take one small action that honors your self-trust—make a clear decision, follow your instincts, or affirm, *I've got me.*

Every step you take is a step toward reclaiming yourself. Forgiveness is ultimately about freedom—not for the one who hurt you, but for *you*. It's a courageous choice to heal, to restore your peace, and to no longer let past wounds define your future.

You deserve the freedom that comes with letting go. Not to excuse the hurt, but to honor your own journey. Remember, forgiveness is not a single act—it's a journey, an unfolding process, and a powerful art form.

The art of trust building empowers you to move forward with strength, wisdom, and a heart that's open to new possibilities.

Navigating Change Using the Seven Steps

Change is a constant in organizational life—teams evolve, strategies shift, structures realign. These shifts are often necessary for growth, but they carry a hidden cost: the vulnerability of trust. Trust doesn't fracture simply because change happens; it fractures when change is handled without care, transparency, or sensitivity to the people it affects.

Poor communication, lack of empathy, and abrupt decisions breed uncertainty. When people don't feel seen or valued, disconnection takes root. And it's in these very moments—when the ground is shifting—that trust becomes most fragile.

When colleagues leave, **relationships are lost**.

When roles shift, **identities are shaken**.

When business cutbacks happen, **opportunities disappear**.

Each of these transitions leaves behind more than just operational gaps—they leave emotional ones. Regardless of how well change is managed, there will be disappointment and loss: the loss of what was and the loss of what might have been. The sense of belonging, purpose, and psychological safety people once relied on begins to erode. These aren't just structural changes; they're deeply human experiences.

And yet, it's in these very moments that leaders have the greatest opportunity—not only to protect trust but to deepen it. The resilience of trust depends entirely on how change is navigated—with honesty, respect, and a steadfast commitment to the human side of transformation.

The Three Dimensions offer a road map for navigating change, and the Seven Steps guide you in helping yourself and others heal from the loss of trust that change can bring. These steps provide a structured pathway for individuals, teams, and organizations to navigate challenges together.

Healing is a process of introspection, inquiry, and discovery. It helps people name concerns, make sense of their loss, rebuild trust, and reconnect—with themselves and with each other. Whether you're leading a team or supporting a colleague, you can draw upon the Seven Steps to foster understanding, rebuild relationships, and help others move forward with new insight into themselves and life.

To begin, embrace these guiding principles:

Be fully present. Show up with authenticity and undivided attention. Let your team feel seen, heard, and valued in every moment.

Demonstrate genuine curiosity. Engage with people beyond their roles. Be curious about their thoughts, feelings, and experiences. True curiosity builds deeper trust and connection.

Go beyond the surface. Move past small talk. Create space for real conversations where teammates can share their concerns, stories, and needs openly and honestly.

By weaving the Reina Seven Steps for Healing into your life—your teamwork, your leadership, your family and friendships—you create spaces where people feel seen, supported, and empowered to grow through change. You foster deeper relationships and equip yourself—and those around you—to meet challenges with strength, confidence, and purpose.

This chapter has explored the emotional weight of broken trust and offered a pathway toward healing. Betrayal brings pain. It can also be a profound teacher. When we're willing to do the inner work, it reveals unexpected gifts: greater self-awareness, deeper resilience, and stronger connection.

Through healing, you don't just rebuild trust—you grow stronger in who you are and in how you show up. When you choose to move forward with an open heart, you transform pain into purpose—and loss into lasting strength. The choices you make today create your tomorrow.

Throughout this book, you've been invited to look inward—to practice the Three Cs with courage, to meet the breakdown of trust with compassion, and to honor the part of you that truly knows relationships.

From this *art of trust building*, something deeper begins to take root: a quiet, unwavering conviction to build, protect, and live trust in every relationship you touch. And from that conviction, transformation emerges.

In the next chapter, we explore *Transformative Trust*—trust as a way of being that elevates culture, deepens connection, and creates lasting change.

CHAPTER SEVEN

The Ripple Effect

Transforming Relationships through Trust

Life's most persistent and urgent question is,
"What are you doing for others?"
MARTIN LUTHER KING JR.

For years, Anna watched her department fall into the same toxic patterns—dismissed ideas, silenced voices, and leadership that ignored concerns. She kept her head down—until the day of a meeting where Thiago, a junior colleague, bravely shared a thoughtful strategy to improve workflow.

When the department head shut down the idea without discussion, Anna saw the impact on Thiago: frustration, retreat, the beginning of doubt. But something shifted within her. She spoke up.

"This addresses the exact problems we've been facing," she said, challenging the unspoken rule of silence.

At first, the room was still. Then one voice joined her. Then another. Together, they created a ripple effect—one that made space for Thiago to speak again and for his idea to be reconsidered.

It wasn't a sweeping victory, but it marked the beginning of change. In that moment, Anna realized that trust is built not just through principles but through courageous, everyday actions.

You've explored the Dimensions of Trust, a powerful framework for cultivating trust through consistent, intentional behaviors. These dimensions equip you with the daily practices needed to build and sustain trust over time—in yourself and in others. Yet even with the best intentions, trust can falter. In moments of pressure, uncertainty, or human missteps, cracks can appear; yet breakdowns are not signs of failure—they're invitations.

When those cracks are met with the courage to deepen connection, trust can transform. It emerges when the Three Dimensions of Trust are practiced in concert with the Seven Steps for Healing. As these approaches are woven together, trust does more than recover; it evolves—becoming stronger, more resilient, and more authentic than before. This is the transformative power of trust that creates ripples that extend outward from your heart to your family, friends, community, team, and even entire organizations.

Like a healthy, flourishing ecosystem, when trust reaches a certain tipping point, it begins growing exponentially, becoming a self-generating and synergistic force that transforms the way people connect and work together. When this coherence occurs, trust integrates seamlessly into daily interactions. It just becomes part of how things flow, changing the way individuals and teams relate to one another and pursue their goals.

This tipping point is called **Transformative Trust**.[1]

The power of Transformative Trust lies in its ability to elevate relationships through acknowledgment, respect, and shared purpose. It acts as a guiding force, encouraging people to lead with intention and act for the greater good.

In trusted relationships, individuals feel empowered, teams grow stronger, and extraordinary outcomes become possible. And from this way of being, Transformative Trust (figure 11) emerges.

Transformative Trust begins when trust shifts from something you *do* to something you *live*. It's not just about actions—it's about presence. This kind of trust transforms how you see yourself, how you relate to others, and how you show up in the world. It reshapes relationships, cultures, and the way you lead.

But this kind of transformation doesn't happen overnight. It unfolds in stages—each building on the last, like stepping stones that carry us from inward reflection to outward impact.

It starts with **courage**—the decision to face yourself honestly and take the first step, even when it's hard. From that place of vulnerability, **compassion** grows. Compassion deepens your empathy, allowing you to connect more fully with others.

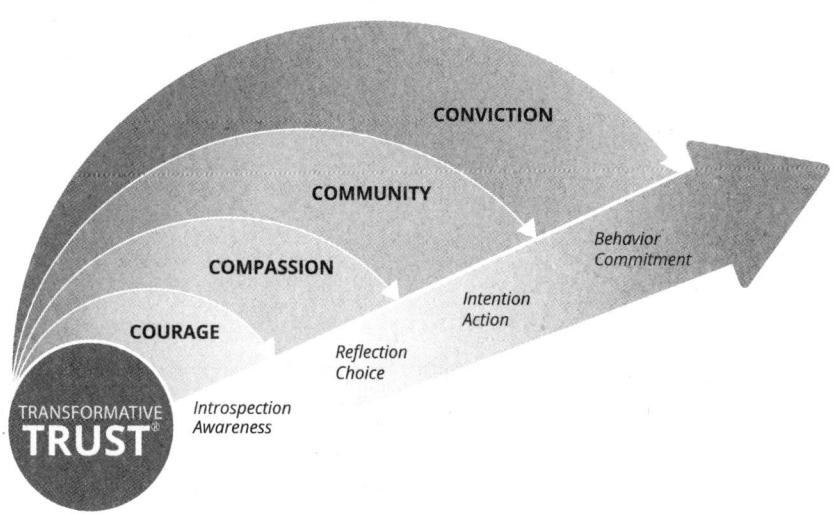

Figure 11. Transformative Trust

As compassion extends outward, you begin to build **community**—spaces where trust and belonging take root. Within true community, you don't just connect—you grow together, support one another, and co-create trust in real time.

And when courage, compassion, and community are woven into the way you live and lead, they give rise to something even deeper: **conviction**. Conviction is the quiet strength that keeps us grounded. It fuels integrity, aligns you with your values, and brings consistency to how you show up—especially when it matters most.

Together, these four characteristics create a foundation for living trust from the *inside out*. They become not just principles, but companions—guiding how we build trust moment by moment, relationship by relationship. This is the essence of Transformative Trust: trust that is lived, embodied, and sustained. It is present in action. And it has the power to shape how you work, live, and lead—every single day.

Courage: The Willingness to Look Within

Transformation begins with courage—the willingness to look inward. It's through honest introspection that you raise your self-awareness and begin to recognize the patterns that influence how you show up in the world.

Your trust building journey starts here. It begins with the quiet invitation to examine your beliefs, your behaviors, and your blind spots. Inner work isn't easy—but it's where growth starts. Choosing to look within is one of the most courageous steps you can take.

At its core, courage means speaking your truth and acting with integrity—even in the presence of fear and uncertainty. It doesn't mean the absence of fear—it means the ability to acknowledge it, honor it, and choose to move forward anyway. The word "courage" comes from the French word *coeur*, meaning "heart," reminding us that true courage stems from within. It is the foundation for trusting yourself—and building trust with others.

As Nelson Mandela said, *Courage is not the absence of fear, but the triumph over it.*[2] That triumph shows up in small and significant moments: when you admit a mistake, confront a betrayal, deliver difficult news, or take ownership of a painful truth. In these moments, courage transforms fear into clarity, vulnerability into strength, and conflict into connection.

Former baseball player, talk show host, and author Lou Vickery put it simply: *Don't minimize the fear. Honor it. Then move forward.*[3] Courage allows you to do just that—not by avoiding discomfort, but by using it as fuel for learning, leadership, and transformation.

In the workplace, courage is essential. It enables you to face ambiguity with curiosity rather than resistance, lead with transparency, and act with authenticity. It gives you the strength to support others in their growth and to model accountability—even when it's uncomfortable.

And when trust has been broken, it is courage that makes healing possible. Owning your part, opening the door to honest dialogue, and extending or receiving forgiveness require vulnerability—but also offer the possibility of deeper, more resilient trust.

Courage expands what's possible. It unlocks self-trust, empowers others, and builds the foundation for meaningful relationships, bold leadership, and transformative change. A snapshot of courage in action can be found in the story of Louie Zamperini:

> *Louie Zamperini's life is a testament to the power of courage, resilience, and self-trust. A troubled youth turned Olympic athlete, Zamperini survived unimaginable hardships during World War II, including twenty-nine days adrift at sea followed by years of relentless torture as a Japanese POW. His resourcefulness and strong will enabled him to endure and overcome challenges that would have broken most others.[4]*
>
> *Perhaps most inspiring is Zamperini's journey from anger and bitterness toward his captors to finding peace via forgiveness. It was through that inner conviction that he set himself free—reminding us that even the most profound pain can become a path to healing, deepened self-trust, and growth.*

Louie's story reminds us that courage isn't a single act—it's a series of everyday choices. The following powerful lessons in courage invite you to recognize, practice, and live this quality in your own life.

Own and speak your truth. Honesty, even when uncomfortable, builds credibility and fosters deeper connection. Speaking your truth with humility, clarity, and authenticity is the bedrock of courageous leadership.

> Example: *After a project veers off course, a team member takes responsibility in a meeting—not only for their role in the breakdown but also for how the team's silence created a sense of psychological insecurity. Rather than assigning blame, they open a pathway for more honest dialogue moving forward.*

Move through fear. Fear is often a signal that growth is near. Stepping into discomfort with intention and preparation builds resilience and self-trust.

> Example: *A rising professional, nervous about public speaking, volunteers to present a project update to senior leadership. They prepare thoroughly, seek coaching, and push through the anxiety. Afterward, they reflect on what they learned—and how much they grew.*

Lift others as you lead. Courage isn't just personal—it's relational. It means creating space for others to be seen, heard, and empowered, especially when their voices are overlooked.

> Example: *Noticing a colleague who's hesitant to speak up, a peer offers quiet encouragement, later amplifying that person's idea during a meeting. They also invite them to co-lead a project, helping build both confidence and trust.*

Lead from the heart. When courage is paired with compassion, trust flourishes. You don't need all the answers—you need the willingness to lead with presence, empathy, and integrity.

> Example: *Sensing rising tension within the team, a manager calls a pause—not to force a quick fix, but to acknowledge what's happening. They invite open dialogue, listen without judgment, and model vulnerability. In doing so, they create space for healing and renewed collaboration.*

When you lead with courage, you create the conditions for trust to take root—within yourself and with those around you—fueling growth, healing, and lasting connection.

But courage alone is not enough. To sustain trust, especially in the face of imperfection and pain, we must meet ourselves and others with something just as essential: **compassion**.

Now let's explore how compassion becomes the force that softens fear, repairs disconnection, and keeps trust alive.

Compassion: The Strength to Stay Open

Courage calls us to look within; compassion invites us to stay open—especially when facing pain, disappointment, or imperfection. It's the steady, heart-centered presence that allows us to remain grounded in empathy, even when emotions run high. Where courage initiates the trust building journey, compassion sustains it—creating the emotional space for connection, healing, and growth to unfold.

Compassion begins with self-compassion, which includes the ability to meet yourself with understanding, forgiveness, and encouragement in times of challenge. Far from being a luxury, self-compassion is a necessary foundation for offering genuine empathy and care to others. It is a heart-centered way of being that grounds the work of trust building and fosters deeper, more authentic connection.

Reflection is essential to cultivating compassion. It invites us to pause, examine our internal narratives, and become aware of our emotional responses. Through this reflective practice, we begin to see ourselves with greater clarity and kindness. Reflection transforms judgment into curiosity, shame into grace, and defensiveness into openness. In these quiet moments of introspection, we reconnect with our shared humanity—and from that recognition, compassion flows outward with integrity and intention.

As the Dalai Lama said, *Love and compassion are necessities, not luxuries. Without them, humanity cannot survive.*[5] This truth holds especially firm in the context of trust building. When we pause to reflect, we create space to make intentional choices about how we show up with others. Rather than reacting from habit or fear, we respond from alignment—with presence, care, and courage.

Compassion is not about rescuing or pitying others. It's about meeting people where they are and recognizing them as inherently valuable and capable—even in moments of struggle or imperfection. True compassion invites us to see through another's eyes and respond with empathy and support, even when it's difficult. At its core, compassion honors the wholeness and dignity of others.

From colleagues to family to strangers, compassion becomes transformative when paired with reflection. It asks us to pause and consider: *What if this person is doing the best they can, given their circumstances?* This simple shift in mindset, especially when embraced by leaders and teams, fosters psychological safety, emotional connection, and mutual respect—all essential conditions for trust to grow.

In compassionate environments, people feel seen, supported, and empowered. Leaders who lead with compassion not only build deeper trust but also inspire loyalty, engagement, and resilience—especially in times of uncertainty or stress. Compassion becomes the quiet force that helps people show up for one another when it matters most.

During the 2010 Zheng-Kai Marathon, Jacqueline Nyetipei Kiplimo demonstrated the power of compassion by sacrificing a $10,000 prize and her chance at first place to help a disabled competitor drink water.[6] For miles, she ran alongside her competitor, constantly prioritizing compassion over personal victory. Her actions exemplify how compassion inspires trust and strengthens bonds, even in high-stakes competitive environments.

A compelling photograph captures this extraordinary moment and reflects the compassionate human spirit at its finest. While we were not able to obtain official permission to publish the image in this book, we'd love for you to see it. You can view it by searching "Zheng-Kai Marathon 2010 Jacqueline Kiplimo image."

Compassion has a ripple effect. Studies—including our own research—consistently show that compassionate interactions benefit both the giver and the receiver. They generate trust, foster connection, and create a deeper sense of understanding. When team members lead with compassion, they build psychological safety, inspire loyalty, and encourage openness. The result: stronger teams, healthier communication, and higher performance.

Compassion also fuels personal growth. It strengthens resilience, cultivates confidence, and deepens self-awareness. And, in an environment where trust and collaboration matter, it's vital for everyone—not just leaders—to understand and embody the principles of compassionate connection.

Whether you're offering support to a colleague, navigating conflict, or holding space during someone's difficult moment, the distinctions between compassion, empathy, and sympathy are essential:

- **Compassion** is more than care—it is the willingness to understand someone's pain and take action to support them. It bridges emotional awareness and helpful behavior, transforming connection into support.

- **Empathy** is the ability to emotionally connect with another's experience—to imagine what they are going through and feel with them. Empathy fosters deep connection, but it doesn't always lead to action unless paired with compassion.

- **Sympathy**, while often well-intentioned, expresses concern from a distance. It involves feeling sorry for someone without fully engaging with or understanding their experience.

In the context of trust building, compassion creates emotional resonance (as empathy does) but also invites thoughtful, values-based action. Compassion says: *I see your struggle, I feel it with you, and I'm here to support you.*

The concepts of trust explored so far come to life through everyday moments—both in the workplace and in your personal life. The following examples are powerful lessons in compassion. They illustrate how trust is built and sustained in both professional and personal settings—because in community, we are constantly shifting between the two.

Begin with self-compassion. Trust begins within. When you treat yourself with compassion and understanding, you build the inner resilience to show up honestly with others. Self-compassion forms the foundation for authentic connection.

A team member misses a deadline. Instead of spiraling into self-criticism, they reflect with grace, take ownership, and communicate clearly with their team.

After snapping at their partner during a stressful day, they reflect with compassion, not shame. They own their behavior, apologize sincerely, and offer themselves grace instead of guilt.

By practicing honesty, accountability, and emotional maturity, the team member or the partner reinforces that they can be trusted to take responsibility and grow.

Pause to reflect before you respond. Reflection helps you move from reaction to intention. It creates space to understand what's really needed—and to choose compassion over judgment. Trust grows in that pause.

> *In a tense meeting, someone notices rising frustration. Instead of reacting defensively, they pause, breathe, and ask, "Can you help me understand where you're coming from?"*

> *During a disagreement with a sibling, they feel triggered but choose to pause. After reflection, they respond, "I'm feeling upset, but I want to understand your perspective."*

By listening openly and responding with emotional clarity, they build trust and model respectful communication.

Act with compassion. Feeling for someone isn't enough. Trust is built when care is made visible through action. Compassion means showing up with tangible support.

> *After a tough client call, a colleague looks overwhelmed. Instead of offering a quick "That sucks," a teammate steps in: "I've got some bandwidth—want me to take a few tasks off your plate?"*

> *A friend is going through a breakup. Instead of saying, "Let me know if you need anything," someone drops off their favorite meal and texts, "I'm here for you—want to go for a walk later?"*

These small acts of kindness signal reliability, presence, and genuine care.

Believe in people's strength, even in struggle. True compassion sees people as capable, not broken. Trust deepens when you honor someone's worth and potential—especially during times of challenge.

A manager sees a team member struggling in a new role. Instead of micromanaging, they offer encouragement and say, "This is a stretch, but I believe you're ready. I'll support you."

A parent sees their teenager overwhelmed with school. Instead of rescuing, they say, "I know this is hard—but I also know you'll figure it out. I'm here if you need me."

By expressing belief in others' ability to grow, they strengthen both trust and confidence.

Compassion bridges gaps, builds trust, and supports people through uncertainty and difficulty. This capacity—to reflect, understand, feel, and respond with care—is the heartbeat of trust that endures.

And yet, compassion doesn't exist in isolation. When extended beyond the individual, it becomes the foundation for something even greater: **community**. It's through our shared actions and collective care that trust begins to scale—shaping cultures where people feel safe, valued, and connected.

Let's explore how trust lives and breathes in the spaces between us.

Community: The Space Where Trust Takes Root

Trust may begin within, but it thrives in relationships. Community is where compassion becomes action—where belonging is built and where trust expands from individual intention to collective experience.

Throughout this book, we've explored community not as a place, but as a living field of connection shaped by trust, compassion, and the energy we bring to one another. Within this field, relationships deepen, belonging takes root, and *we* begin to matter more than *I*.

Recognizing that you are part of something greater, whether at work, at home, or in society, inspires you to act with intention. You choose how to show up—not just for yourself, but with an awareness of how your presence impacts the whole: your family, neighbors, friends, and colleagues. Trust is what makes this shift possible. It transforms ordinary roles into meaningful threads within the larger collective and elevates daily interactions into acts of service and connection.

At its most transformative, a community grounded in trust invites openness, honesty, and mutual respect. It creates the conditions for people to take risks, repair disconnects, and co-create without fear. When trust is present, relationships shift from transactional to transformational. Trust becomes the energy that fuels collaboration, nurtures growth, and moves us from *I* to *we*—creating a space where people feel safe to contribute, connect, and thrive.

The reflections that follow offer simple but powerful ways to bring community to life—wherever you are, and in whatever role you hold:

Community thrives when we shift from *I* to *we*. Trust grows when we see ourselves not as separate from others, but as co-creators of a shared experience. Community is strongest when you move from individualism to mutual responsibility.

> *In a neighborhood organizing a cleanup effort, one resident steps up to coordinate resources and invite others—not because they were asked, but because they see the well-being of the group as their own. Others feel inspired to join in, creating a ripple effect of contribution.*

The neighbor acts with initiative and integrity, demonstrating a deep commitment to the collective good.

Belonging begins with welcoming others as they are. People feel they belong not when they are improved or corrected, but when they are truly received. Community deepens when we meet others with curiosity rather than judgment.

> *In a workplace meeting, a manager pauses to ensure every voice is heard—including the quieter team members. Rather than moving on quickly, they say, "We haven't heard from you yet—what are your thoughts?" That moment of inclusion fosters connection, trust, and engagement.*

The manager intentionally invites all voices into the conversation, signaling that everyone is valued exactly as they are.

Trust is strengthened through shared accountability. In healthy communities, accountability is not about control—it's about care and respect. People hold themselves and one another accountable for upholding shared values and commitments.

> *In a volunteer group, a member misses a key responsibility. Instead of blame, the team reflects together on what happened and invites the member to reengage. The message is clear: we trust you to return, and we're in this together.*

The group responds with understanding and shared ownership, reinforcing accountability as a trust building practice.

Purpose becomes powerful when it's shared. Community isn't just about connection—it's about shared intention. When people unite around a common goal, trust becomes the force that carries them through conflict and change.

> *A team launching a new social initiative begins each meeting by revisiting their shared purpose. Even when challenges arise, that shared North Star brings them back to alignment.*

Disagreements are navigated with respect because the purpose (the why) is bigger than any one perspective.

The team grounds each conversation in purpose, allowing trust and common intention to guide them forward.

Community is built through the intentional actions of each person—how we listen, support, and show up for one another. When you contribute with care and purpose, you create the conditions for trust, connection, and shared growth. In doing so, you don't just belong to community—you help bring it to life.

And when you consistently choose to show up this way—again and again, especially when it's hard—something deeper begins to emerge—**conviction**.

Conviction: The Commitment That Sustains Trust

Conviction is what transforms trust from a practice into a way of life. It's the quiet, steady force that anchors your intentions, aligns your actions, and strengthens your presence—no matter the circumstance.

Conviction is born from a deep commitment to relationships—a commitment that, over time, becomes woven into the fabric of who you are. Through the inner work of introspection (courage) and the guiding practice of reflection (compassion), you begin to show up with greater clarity and purpose. You set conscious intentions and take aligned action, demonstrating a devotion to the people and communities you serve (community).

What begins as commitment matures into conviction—a grounded, unshakable way of being. Conviction is not performative or situational; it's embodied and enduring. It is through this journey—from awareness to action, from intention to integrity—that true transformation takes root.

Conviction becomes the foundation of purpose. It defines the "why" behind your actions and anchors you to the values that shape your life. When someone leads with true conviction, it shows in the consistency of their choices, the clarity with which they face challenges, and the integrity woven through their words and actions. These individuals embody trustworthiness, not because they are perfect, but because they live from a grounded understanding of who they are—*and* what they stand for.

By aligning your values with meaningful behavior, conviction cultivates both self-trust and reliability in the eyes of others. It becomes the force that empowers you to embody the Three Dimensions of Trust, embrace the vulnerability trust requires, and walk the Seven Steps for Healing with authenticity. In doing so, you expand your capacity to offer and receive trust, and you build deeper, more resilient relationships.

Ultimately, conviction arises from knowing what matters most and aligning your life with that deeper truth. It becomes the inner light that fuels your decisions each day—the reason you move through the world with intention and the desire to contribute meaningfully. When your actions are rooted in this alignment, they radiate clarity, strength, and a deep sense of purpose.

Conviction to relationships, lived fully, becomes a catalyst for trust. It's the heartbeat of transformative leadership, the anchor for lasting relationships, and the foundation for cultures where trust is not only built—but sustained.

Conviction comes to life through the choices you make—especially when they're hard. Consider these powerful lessons in conviction. These reflections show how aligning action with values builds trust that lasts.

Conviction deepens commitment to trust-based relationships.
Conviction is the evolution of commitment. It transforms intention into a sustained, values-driven way of living. More than a momentary promise, conviction reflects a lasting dedication to protect, repair, and nurture trust-based relationships. With conviction, connection is no longer conditional—it becomes a way of being.

> *After a breach of trust in a close friendship, one friend commits not just to making amends but to rebuilding the relationship through consistent, honest communication and presence. In time, the other friend meets that effort with openness and care. Together, they rebuild trust—step by step, choice by choice.*

> *Similarly, after a long period of emotional distance, a sibling chooses to reconnect—not with a grand gesture, but through small, steady actions: checking in, listening deeply, and being present. Over time, trust is restored and the relationship renewed.*

Conviction shows up—especially when it's hard. Conviction is tested in discomfort. It's easy to stay aligned with your values when the stakes are low and things are going well—but true transformation happens when you uphold those values under pressure.

> *A team member witnessing a colleague being unfairly criticized in a meeting calmly names the impact and advocates for a more respectful dialogue—even at the risk of pushback. This courageous action demonstrates conviction in real time.*

Conviction fuels the discipline to keep showing up. Conviction requires consistency, especially when progress is slow or invisible. It's the daily, deliberate choices that build trust over time.

A parent working through past wounds commits to weekly self-reflection and family check-ins—not to be perfect, but to rebuild trust through steady presence and effort.

Conviction inspires and elevates others. True conviction is contagious. When someone lives with clarity and commitment, it inspires others to act in alignment with their own values.

As a critical deadline approaches, stress runs high and the pressure to cut corners intensifies. The team begins to lose confidence—until the leader steps in. Grounded in their conviction to trust and to relationships, they lean in instead of away. By naming the pressure, inviting honest dialogue, and trusting the team's abilities, the leader models trust in action. Their steady presence guides the group back to focus, integrity, and shared commitment.

Transformative Trust emerges through courage, compassion, community, and conviction—each deepening our capacity to build trust as a way of life. The *art of trust building* becomes a way of being, a way of leading, and a way of leaving an enduring legacy of trust that lives on in every person you touch.

Gratitude is how we honor that transformation. It's the expression of all that trust has cultivated within and between us. Let's now turn to gratitude—the final, sustaining thread in the fabric of trust.

CHAPTER EIGHT

Gratitude in Action

Trust Building through Appreciation

*If the only prayer you ever say in your entire
life is thank you, it will be enough.*
MEISTER ECKHART

Sam was a respected CEO—efficient, composed, and always in control. His biotech team followed his lead and met their goals but offered little beyond what was asked. While things ran smoothly on the surface, Sam sensed something was missing.

Then came a crisis.

A system failure jeopardized a major product launch. Tension rose. Communication slowed. Sam pushed harder, but traction slipped. That's when Meera, a senior engineer, quietly said, "People don't need more pressure. They need to know we're in this together."

Her words stopped him.

Instead of reacting, Sam called the team together—not to give orders, but to listen. He acknowledged the stress, admitted he didn't have all the answers, and asked, "What do you need—from me and from each other—to get through this?"

155

First, silence. Then ideas emerged. Engineers volunteered to pair up. The quality assurance team offered extra hours. Communication gaps were bridged. The room shifted from tension to collaboration. They weren't just fixing a problem— they were owning the solution.

The launch crossed the finish line, but the real transformation came after—gratitude, laughter, renewed energy. The appreciation wasn't directed at Sam; it was shared among the team. They felt seen, heard, and trusted. For the first time, Sam experienced a deeper kind of success, not from directing people, but from empowering them.

Sam finally understood: Trust isn't earned through power; it grows through presence—and gratitude is what makes that presence known, valued, and shared.

The experience fundamentally transformed Sam's approach to leadership. He no longer saw appreciation as a nice gesture. Instead, it became core to how he led.

He began opening meetings by spotlighting individual contributions, not just metrics. He wrote handwritten thank-you notes to team members who went above and beyond, often sharing their efforts publicly to amplify their impact. He paused in hallways to express genuine thanks, asked deeper questions in one-on-one meetings, and made space in team reflections to celebrate not just wins, but the people behind them.

Over time, this shift in behavior created a ripple effect. Gratitude became contagious. People felt seen and valued, not just for what they delivered, but for who they were. They began offering bold ideas, backing each other up without being asked, and showing up with renewed energy. Trust wasn't just growing—it was becoming the culture.

Months later, George, a longtime team lead, smiled and said, "I don't think I've ever seen the team this connected." With a full heart, Sam nodded. He understood now that trust isn't forged through authority or outcomes alone; it's cultivated through everyday moments of gratitude and appreciation—consistently given and genuinely felt.

This story reveals the power of gratitude in trust building. When people feel seen and appreciated, they don't just follow—they engage, contribute, and give their best. True leadership isn't about commanding results; it's about creating an environment where people feel valued and inspired to do their best work.

Gratitude is commonly defined as "appreciative of benefits received; expressing thankfulness; or bringing contentment or joy." But beyond these definitions, gratitude is far more than a mental concept—it's a felt experience.

Before moving on, take a moment to slow down and read the following quotes—not just with your analytical mind, but with your heart. Let them gently land in your awareness without interpretation:

The best way to show my gratitude is to accept everything, even my problems, with joy.
MOTHER TERESA

Gratitude is not only the greatest of virtues, but the parent of all others.
CICERO

Gratitude can transform common days into thanksgivings, turn routine jobs into joy, and change ordinary opportunities into blessings.
THEODORE ROOSEVELT

We can only be said to be alive in those moments
when our hearts are conscious of our treasures.
THORNTON WILDER

One looks back with appreciation to the brilliant
teachers, but with gratitude to those who touched
our human feelings . . . but warmth is the vital element
for the growing plant and for the soul of the child.
CARL JUNG

What do these voices—spanning from saint to statesman, philosopher to psychologist, and playwright to president—have in common?

They speak to the deeper truth: gratitude is not just a feeling—it's a transformative force. It sustains your conviction to relationships and fuels lasting transformative trust. It turns transactions into relationships, and relationships into community. From this space, authentic trust, deeper connections, and meaningful growth emerge.

Though gratitude, appreciation, and love are intangible, they are anything but invisible. These energies are felt viscerally and unmistakably through the senses—living forces that move through us. As emotions (*energy in motion*), they radiate from the heart, transcending time and space while touching others, often speaking louder than words.

These powerful currents of human connection resonate with the abundant rhythm of the universe itself. They remind us that what's most real isn't always seen—but it's *always* felt. When we lead from the emotions of the heart, we don't just build relationships—we elevate them.

When genuinely cultivated, gratitude and appreciation elevate your energetic state, naturally attracting blessings, opportunities, and positive experiences. Imagine it being like tuning in to your favorite radio station—the clearer the signal, the stronger the reception.

Throughout this chapter, we will explore the *art of trust building* through these facets:

- The ripple effect of gratitude: building relationships through appreciation

- Gratitude as a catalyst for resilience, creativity, and connection

What you're likely to discover is that when you practice gratitude as a way of being—not just a polite gesture or empty routine—it catalyzes a ripple effect that reaches far beyond the moment. Practiced with sincerity, gratitude strengthens workplace relationships, deepens family bonds, and fosters cohesion in teams and communities.

Like trust, gratitude is naturally reciprocal. It lifts others—and lifts you in return—reinforcing connection and mutual trust. But what sustains those relationships over time isn't gratitude alone. It's your unwavering conviction to those relationships, a characteristic of *Transformative Trust*, which we explored in chapter 7.

Conviction to relationships goes beyond care. It's the unwavering commitment to prioritize, protect, and invest in the relationship itself. Gratitude becomes one of the most powerful ways we embody that conviction. It says, *I see you and value you. I'm choosing this relationship—not out of need, but out of belief in its worth.*

The Ripple Effect of Gratitude

Gratitude is a transformative force that creates a ripple effect of positivity and serves as the mechanism by which trust deepens and connections strengthen. At its core, gratitude is a powerful recognition of care and love. While many believe love has no place in business or leadership, experience and research show otherwise. Teams built on genuine appreciation, respect, and care consistently inspire higher levels of trust, loyalty, and performance.

A powerful example of this in action can be found at Buurtzorg, a successful home healthcare organization in the Netherlands.[1] At Buurtzorg, employees are trusted to manage their schedules, make decisions collaboratively, and work without traditional hierarchies. This culture of autonomy, appreciation, and shared purpose has fueled outstanding outcomes—especially among younger generations like Gen Z, who prioritize meaningful work and human-centered leadership.[2]

Driven by a passion to make a positive impact because they feel empowered and appreciated, Buurtzorg staff consistently go above and beyond for their patients, not just addressing medical needs but also caring for the whole person. The result? Lower healthcare costs, better patient outcomes, and stronger relationships across the organization—and science backs it up.

Research shows that practicing gratitude contributes to the following outcomes:

- Lifting moods and reducing depression

- Strengthening relationships and trust

- Lowering inflammation and easing anxiety

- Boosting energy and improving sleep

- Building resilience during tough times

- Enhancing overall emotional and physical well-being

Gratitude, when embedded in how you lead and live, doesn't just feel good—it works.

Gratitude as a Catalyst

Gratitude has the unique power to transform challenges into opportunities for resilience, creativity, and connection. When cultivated over time, such authentic gratitude possesses the power to transform one's mindset from a victim mentality to that of a creator. Take, for example, Mohammed:

> *After a series of setbacks—including a failed product launch and the unexpected exit of a key investor—Mohammed was hit hardest by a deeper blow: his longtime business partner betrayed him by withdrawing from their venture and taking clients. The financial strain was heavy, but the rupture in trust shook Mohammed's confidence in his own judgment.*
>
> *Rather than bypass the pain, Mohammed turned to the Seven Steps for Healing as a lifeline (see chapter 6). He moved through each step with honesty—acknowledging the loss, honoring his disappointment, and leaning on the support of loved ones who reflected his resilience back to him.*
>
> *Through deep introspection, he recognized how urgency had led him to override his instincts, compromise his judgment, and miss the early warning signs of misalignment. With time, gratitude began to surface—not for the betrayal, but for what it revealed. The experience gave Mohammed a chance to slow down, recalibrate, and rebuild with clarity, alignment, and conviction. In the end, the greatest gift wasn't just healing—it was rediscovering what success meant on his own terms.*

While Mohammed would not want to relive those experiences of loss, he carried with him gratitude for the lessons and insights gained:

Trust starts within. Mohammed learned that true leadership begins with self-trust. He became grateful for the reminder that when you listen deeply to your intuition—especially in moments of doubt—you stay rooted in integrity, even when outcomes are uncertain.

Setbacks are invitations, not endings. What once felt like failure became an opportunity for realignment. Mohammed grew thankful for the insights that his challenges redirected him toward, ones that were more authentic and sustainable.

Urgency is not the same as clarity. He realized he had been chasing success out of urgency, not alignment. He became grateful for the chance to slow down, clarify his vision, and move forward with intention rather than pressure.

Discernment is a form of wisdom. The betrayal taught Mohammed to pay closer attention to early warning signs. He became grateful for the painful experience that sharpened his discernment and deepened his ability to choose partnerships more consciously.

Values are the foundation of meaningful work. In rebuilding, Mohammed surrounded himself with people who shared his values—not just his goals. He became grateful for the deeper sense of fulfillment that comes from working in alignment with people he trusts and respects.

Resilience is built through support. He recognized the power of quiet, consistent support from loved ones during his lowest moments. He became grateful for the realization that strength isn't about going it alone but about allowing yourself to lean on others when needed.

Success is redefined through healing. Finally, Mohammed became grateful for the space to redefine what success means to him—not just achievement, but wholeness, purpose, and alignment with his true self.

Gratitude didn't erase the pain, but it gave him a new lens—one that helped him rebuild not only his business but his self-trust.

Mohammed's story is a powerful reminder that when trust breaks down—especially in painful, personal ways—gratitude can be the thread that helps you mend. It strengthens your relationship with yourself and fuels the perseverance needed to rise again with greater wisdom and resilience.

Like Mohammed, we too have experienced the highs, lows, wins, and heartbreaks that come with building a business and navigating relationships across all areas of life. And like Mohammed, we've learned to be grateful for the wisdom each moment offers. Every challenge and every triumph has deepened our conviction, fueling the work we bring into the world.

For more than three and a half decades at our company, this perspective has been at the heart of everything we do. It brings us immense gratitude and joy to know that our trust building work has helped transform individuals, teams, and organizations to create cultures rooted in authenticity and connection. What moves us most is when these changes ripple beyond the workplace—healing families, strengthening personal relationships, and inspiring new ways of being. The gratitude we've experienced in serving others has been both a profound privilege and a guiding force in the work we continue to do.

Now here's the good news: incorporating gratitude into daily life is easier than you think. As an example, try this: each day, write down three things you're grateful for. Place the list somewhere visible (on your refrigerator or mirror, next to your bed, or on an office wall), and revisit it whenever frustration or negativity creeps in.

This simple practice can shift your perspective, reminding you of life's blessings while helping you refocus on positivity. What you will find is that with consistent effort, gratitude becomes a natural and transformative habit, enriching your relationships and bolstering your resilience.

The Art of Expressing Gratitude

Research consistently shows that gratitude contributes to greater happiness and emotional well-being. As Robert A. Emmons, a leading gratitude researcher, notes, *The practice of gratitude can have dramatic and lasting effects in a person's life.*[3]

As an example, gratitude lowers blood pressure, improves immune function, and reduces the risk of depression, anxiety, and substance abuse. It's also a powerful resilience factor, helping individuals navigate adversity and prevent burnout.

As we've seen and experienced, gratitude isn't just a feeling—it's a practice—a way of affirming value, fostering self-trust, and deepening the relationships that matter most. Whether you're navigating the ups and downs of business, healing from personal challenges, or simply wanting to lead with more heart, expressing gratitude can shift the energy of any moment—for yourself and for others.

So how and where do you begin?

You start now, right where you are. Begin by speaking words of appreciation to yourself and those around you. In both personal and professional contexts, gratitude is a powerful tool for building meaningful connections.

To help you get started, here are a few heartfelt expressions of gratitude you can share with coworkers, friends, family, and loved ones to convey your sincere appreciation:

I appreciate you. Simple, direct, and heartfelt—this phrase carries weight because it affirms the person, not just their actions.

You bring your heart and soul to this team. This is a powerful way to recognize someone's impact and presence—not just what they do, but who they are.

I am a better person because of you. This expression elevates gratitude by acknowledging transformation and personal growth inspired by the other.

I thank you for your commitment. This is a sincere acknowledgment of dedication, showing emotional depth and recognition.

You have taught me so much. Gratitude for wisdom, experience, and mentorship honors the value of what someone has shared.

No words can express, no act of gratitude can relay, no gift can represent, what your love and support have meant to me. Deeply moving, this expression conveys profound appreciation when ordinary thanks doesn't feel sufficient.

I value your wisdom. These words recognize not just knowledge, but the insight and perspective someone brings, which is especially powerful in relationships and leadership.

You can count on me. A reciprocal gesture of gratitude can turn appreciation into action and trust.

I trust you. Few expressions carry more weight—this one communicates both appreciation and emotional safety.

Someday, I hope to give you a fraction of all you've given me. This is a humble, heartfelt way to express deep gratitude and the desire to give back.

These phrases are not just empty words but, rather, bridges that deepen trust and connection, especially during times of uncertainty or challenge.

When you take small yet meaningful steps, such as saying, *I appreciate you*, or offering a simple *How can I help?*—you're trust building. Gratitude reassures people that their efforts and presence are valued, fostering confidence and a sense of belonging.

Mastering the Art of Expressing Gratitude

Gratitude is more than a fleeting emotion; it's a deliberate practice that expands trust in yourself and in others. By focusing on specific and authentic expressions of appreciation, you create a ripple effect of trust in both personal and professional relationships. Here are actionable strategies to help you master incorporating gratitude into your life:

Start with yourself. Write down three things you're grateful for each day. Practicing gratitude privately—through journaling or affirmations—builds self-trust and rewires your mindset for positivity. Over time, you'll notice an increase in intuitive abilities and emotional resilience.

Express it out loud. Tell someone you appreciate them and explain why. Write a note or send a quick text.

Acknowledging the impact of others strengthens relationships and reminds you of the support you have in your network. This practice boosts confidence and deepens mutual trust.

Turn challenges into teachers. Ask yourself, *What is this experience here to teach me?* Gratitude during adversity expands your perspective, builds resilience, and helps you grow stronger through life's inevitable ups and downs.

Be present with the good. Pause daily to savor something simple—a kind word, a meal, a moment of peace. Whether it's savoring your morning coffee or watching the sunset, focus on the positive. Practicing mindfulness through gratitude increases self-awareness, captures intuitive nudges, and cultivates peace and contentment.

Make it a shared practice. Create moments to share gratitude with others, such as your partner, team, or family. Whether it's a dinner table ritual or a team check-in, by sharing what you're thankful for, you strengthen your bond and reinforce mutual trust. This habit fosters positivity and enhances your role as a supportive partner.

When challenges and setbacks arise—and they will—remember that gratitude is one of the most powerful forces for transformation. It rebuilds trust, fuels resilience, and deepens the connections that sustain us through difficulty. When practiced consistently, gratitude becomes more than a feeling—it becomes a way of being that aligns with the heart of Transformative Trust. By weaving gratitude into your daily life, you reinforce your conviction to your relationships and strengthen the foundation for trust that endures—within yourself and with those around you.

As we close this exploration of gratitude, we come full circle. You've walked the path of trust—from its foundations to its fragility, from personal practice to cultural transformation. Along the way, you've been invited to reflect, to feel, to lead with presence, and to choose relationships with intention. You've seen how trust is built, how it can break, and how it can be rebuilt and renewed.

Next, in the conclusion, we'll bring it all together.

Conclusion

The Art of Trust Building

Your Path Forward

As we reach the conclusion of *The Art of Trust Building*, one truth becomes clear: **trust is not a destination but a way of being— lived moment by moment, relationship by relationship.**

Trust building is both a practice and an art—a living, breathing process shaped by awareness, intention, and meaningful connection. It is the invisible thread that runs through every relationship, adding depth to how we lead, how we live, and how we love.

Throughout this book, you've explored the many dimensions of trust: how it begins within, how it's strengthened through behavior, how it can fracture, and how it can be healed. You've learned that trust is not a single act, but a rhythm—a choice made again and again. It asks us to show up with courage, extend compassion, build community, and live with conviction.

You've seen that trust is more than just a mindset. It's energy. It flows through how you speak to yourself, how you treat others, and your willingness to be present in the moments that matter. It doesn't require perfection—only your willingness to lead with presence and care.

Trust building is legacy work. It's not something you achieve once, but something you live—choice by choice, conversation by conversation. Each act of honesty, kindness, and humility becomes a brushstroke on the canvas of your life. And when you invite others into that creative process, you co-create something greater than yourself: a shared masterpiece of human connection.

Trust is not the imprint of power—it's the imprint of presence. And it's yours to leave everywhere you go.

Trust Building in Action

No matter where you are on your trust building journey—whether you're rebuilding trust, deepening it, or learning to extend it more freely—what matters most is that you begin.

The steps that follow are here to meet you exactly where you are. Each one is designed to help you take intentional, meaningful action—one choice, one moment, one relationship at a time. Because trust is built not through grand gestures, but through consistent, everyday practice.

This is your invitation to begin. Use these Ten Trust Building Actions to live *The Art of Trust Building* every day:

1. Claim your trustworthiness. Before you can build trust with others, you must first recognize the trust that already lives within you. Yet in times of stress, conflict, or self-doubt, it's easy to forget the qualities that make us trustworthy. This practice is about remembering and reconnecting with the values and intentions that guide how you show up.

Here is how to begin.

Create a quiet space to reflect. Tune into yourself with honesty and compassion. Then, write down three truths about yourself that make you trustworthy. For example, *I speak truthfully and with care in my interactions.* These are your anchor points. Keep them close. They will serve as your inner compass when trust feels fragile or when you need to return to your center.

When you claim your trustworthiness, you stand on solid ground. Even in moments of vulnerability, these truths remind you of who you are—and who you are becoming.

Reflection:

- *What qualities make me trustworthy—even when I forget them?*

- *Which of my values or actions helps others feel safe, supported, or seen?*

- *How might I return to these truths when I begin to doubt myself?*

2. Set one trust-centered intention each day. Life moves fast. You likely find yourself moving from one demand to the next, responding, reacting, and navigating deadlines and distractions. In the busyness of it all, it's easy to lose sight of your deeper intentions. You become consumed by the *doingness* of the day, while the *beingness*— the presence you bring to your relationships—gets left behind.

This step invites you to pause. To create a little room at the start of your day to align with how you want to show up.

Here is how to begin.

Each morning, take a few quiet minutes to review your day ahead. What conversations or moments of connection lie ahead? Then ask yourself: *How do I want to bring myself* *to these interactions?* Choose one trust-centered intention—something simple and true. For example: *Today, I will bring curiosity instead of judgment.* Let that intention guide your actions throughout the day—not as pressure, but as alignment and as a quiet anchor. This is how trust is built—one intentional moment at a time.

Reflection:

■ *What kind of energy do I typically bring into my day, and is it aligned with who I want to be?*

■ *What relationship could I approach with more intention?*

3. Reinforce self-trust with positive self-talk. Trust begins with the way you speak to yourself. When the pressure is on—when mistakes happen, plans shift, or uncertainty creeps in—it's easy to turn inward with criticism or doubt. Vulnerability rises, and your inner voice can become harsh or unforgiving. But these moments call for grace, not judgment.

This step is about choosing compassion over self-criticism. It's about remembering the truth of who you are—and reinforcing that truth when it feels furthest from reach.

Here is how to begin.

The next time you feel uncertain, discouraged, or vulnerable, pause and shift your internal dialogue. Instead of focusing on what's wrong, speak to yourself as you would to someone you care about. Say: *I am committed to learning. I am a work in progress—and that's OK. I am gaining strength.* Keep these words nearby. Say them out loud. Let them guide you back to your center.

Trust building starts by offering yourself the same grace you want to extend to others. When your inner voice reflects compassion, your outer presence radiates strength—and trust takes root from the inside out.

Reflect on a moment when you were hard on yourself, then ask:

- *What would it have looked like to respond with kindness instead of criticism?*

- *What words of encouragement could I offer myself right now?*

Take a moment to write down your words, and revisit them when you need to return to your inner foundation of trust.

4. Follow through on one commitment—no matter how small.
We've all been there. You make a commitment—fully intending to follow through—but life happens. The urgency of other demands takes over. The task lingers in your mind, creating a quiet sense of pressure or guilt. Even if the other person hasn't followed up, you carry the weight of that unfulfilled promise.

And while the delay may seem small, these moments matter. Because trust isn't just built through big gestures—it's maintained in the smallest acts of follow-through.

Here's how to begin.

Think of one promise, agreement, or commitment you've made to someone—something that hasn't been completed yet, even if it feels minor. Then, reach out. If you're able to fulfill it now, do so—and let them know it matters to you. If you need more time, ask to revisit or revise the agreement together. Be honest. Offer a new timeline and be sure you're both aligned.

This simple act—*naming the commitment and staying in communication*—can preserve or even strengthen trust. It tells the other person, you matter. I haven't forgotten. I'm still holding this with care.

Trust isn't about being flawless. It's about being accountable. And sometimes, the smallest follow-through becomes the biggest signal that you can be counted on.

Reflection:

- *Is there a commitment—personal or professional—that's been quietly weighing on me?*

- *What would shift if I simply reached out today?*

- *What might it restore—in my relationship and in myself?*

5. Resolve a misstep that may be lingering. We've all had moments when we didn't show up as the person we intended to be. Maybe we spoke too quickly, stayed silent when we should have spoken up, or missed an opportunity to follow through. In the rush of life, it's easy to move on and push these moments aside—but unresolved missteps don't always fade. They tend to linger—in our minds, in our relationships, and in the space between us and others.

You may still think about a moment where your actions didn't reflect your values. You meant well, but something fell short. That unsettled feeling is often a quiet signal: *there's still something here that wants to be repaired.* This step is about responding to that signal.

Here's how to begin.

Think of a moment—recent or distant—when you wish you had shown up differently. It might be something small, like not responding in time or missing a cue to offer support. Or perhaps it's something more significant, like overlooking someone's input or delaying a hard conversation. Then take one step to reconnect. Acknowledge the moment. Express your desire to repair it. Offer a sincere apology if needed— and reaffirm that the relationship matters to you. It doesn't have to be perfect. What matters is that you show up with humility and heart.

Repair is one of the most powerful trust building behaviors you have. Because when you take ownership, you don't just mend the moment—you strengthen the relationship.

Reflection:

- *What moment—however small—still lingers?*

- *What truth needs to be spoken to clear the air or close the loop?*

6. Have one truth-telling conversation. Trust deepens when we allow others to see more of who we are. There may be something you've been carrying—an unspoken truth, an appreciation left unsaid, a boundary not yet voiced. Perhaps it's been lingering quietly, waiting for the right moment. This step is your invitation to stop waiting and to open the door to deeper connection.

When we share something meaningful, we let others in—not just into the conversation, but into our hearts. And it's often these honest, heart-centered moments that become turning points in relationships.

Here's how to begin.

Reach out to someone for whom trust matters. It might be a colleague, a friend, a partner, or a teammate. Then, with care and intention, express something real. You might say: *I'd like to share something with you that's been on my mind.* You don't need to overexplain or get it perfect. You simply need to speak from your truth—with humility, courage, and care.

Truth telling is an invitation. It says: *I trust you enough to let you in.* And that trust—extended vulnerably and freely— creates a foundation for authentic relationships to flourish.

Reflection:

- *What truth, appreciation, or need have I held back that could open the door to deeper trust?*

- *What's one conversation I could have today that would bring more honesty into this relationship?*

7. Offer compassion to someone who let you down. When trust is shaken, compassion becomes a powerful choice. Maybe someone dropped the ball. Broke a promise. Left you out. Said nothing when you needed support. It's easy to retreat into judgment or distance when we're disappointed—especially when we expected more.

But before you assume intent, this step invites you to pause and consider the possibility of something deeper. When someone falls short, ask yourself:

- *Is this a one-time misstep or part of a pattern?*

- *Might they be carrying something I can't see?*

- *Have I ever struggled in a similar way?*

- *What would I want if the roles were reversed?*

This is not about excusing harmful behavior—it's about soften-
ing the rigidity of assumption and making space for understanding. Compassion doesn't mean you ignore impact. It means you
respond with presence and care, even when you're hurting.

Here's how to begin.

**Think of someone who has recently disappointed or let
you down.** Consider reaching out with curiosity and kindness. You might say:

- *Can I check in with you about something?*

- *I noticed you seemed distant, and I've been wondering if
  something's going on.*

These small acts build trust in moments where disconnection could easily take hold. And even if you don't speak to
the person directly, simply choosing to view them with compassion can create space for healing.

Reflection:

- *What assumptions am I making—and what might I not know?*

- *What would compassion look like in this situation?*

**8. Have a relationship check-in with someone important to
you.** Relationships are at the heart of a meaningful life. We don't
live in isolation. The most precious part of our lives isn't what
we do—but who we share it with. And yet, in the rhythm of daily
life, it's easy to assume that the people closest to us know how

much we care. That the trust between us is solid. That things are "fine."

But trust should never be taken for granted. It deserves care. Attention. And moments of reflection. This step invites you to check in with someone who matters. A partner, a friend, a colleague, or a family member. Not because something is wrong, but because the relationship matters to you—and you want to keep it strong.

Here's how to begin.

Reach out with intention. You might say:

- *I care about our relationship; can we take a few minutes to reflect on how we're supporting one another?*

- *How can we work together to keep our connection strong and healthy?*

And most importantly—**listen**. With curiosity, not defensiveness. With care, not control. The goal isn't to fix, impress, or perform. It's to understand. To stay aligned. To grow together.

Reflection:

- *Who do I want to feel more connected to?*

- *What might they need from me right now—and how can I show them they matter?*

9. Extend gratitude to others. Trust grows stronger when we take the time to name and honor it. Every day, you experience small moments where trust is alive—in a colleague's honesty, a friend's presence, a partner's support, or even a stranger's kindness. These moments matter. They shape your relationships, ease your path, and often go unnoticed in the rush of life.

But gratitude turns these moments into something more. It tells someone, *I see you. I see what you did—and the difference it made.*

Here's how to begin.

Think of a recent moment when someone showed up with integrity, courage, kindness, or support—something that helped you move forward, feel seen, or feel safe. Then, express your gratitude directly. You might say: *I want to thank you for the way you listened. It made a difference.* Extend that gratitude inward as well. Acknowledge your own presence in the relationship. What did you contribute?

Gratitude is a relational amplifier. It strengthens what's already good, and it reinforces the flow of trust between people.

Reflection:

- *Whose presence, action, or support made a difference for me recently?*

- *Have I told them?*

10. Revisit the Reina Individual Trust Scale. Growth begins with awareness—and it continues with intention. At the beginning of this book, you were invited to take the *Reina Individual Trust Scale Assessment* to reflect on how you show up in trust building relationships. That tool was designed to serve you—to help you see yourself and your behaviors more fully, so you can lead with purpose, awareness, and heart.

If you haven't yet taken the assessment, now is the perfect moment. Head to the Resources section of this book for guidance, and complete the assessment with honesty and curiosity. Let it show you where your energy, attention, and intention might be most powerfully directed.

And if you *have* already taken it—and some time has passed— consider taking it again. Use it as a mirror to recognize your growth, revisit your patterns, and renew your commitment to the *art of trust building.*

This is your invitation to step forward with clarity.

To deepen self-trust.

To strengthen relationships.

To live with presence and purpose—every day.

A Way Forward in Trust

Each of these steps is simple in form—but profound in impact.

Trust isn't built on grand declarations. It lives in the small, daily moments of awareness, intention, and care. When you practice even one of these actions, you reinforce the foundation of trust—within yourself and with others.

Come back to these steps whenever you feel disconnected, uncertain, or ready to deepen your relationships. Let them meet you where you are. Let them grow with you as you grow.

Because trust isn't something you check off a list.

It's something you *live*—choice by choice, conversation by conversation, moment by meaningful moment.

And that's how the *art of trust building* becomes a way of life.

A Final Invitation

As you step beyond these pages, remember:

The art of trust building lives in you.

In your choices.

In your courage.

In your compassion.

In your conviction to relationships that matter.

Let your presence be your legacy.

Let trust be the imprint you leave—wherever you go.

From Our Hearts to Yours

As we close this book, please know this is not goodbye.

This is a shared beginning.

The journey of trust building is not linear or perfect.

It's tender. It's real. And it unfolds moment by moment, step by step, choice by choice.

We want you to know **you're not walking it alone.**

We're on this path with you—learning, stumbling, growing, and beginning again. Just like you, we are continually practicing the art of trust building in our lives, our relationships, and the spaces we're honored to hold.

Thank you for letting us be a part of your journey.

Thank you for your courage, your heart, and your willingness to show up.

May trust guide your steps.

May love fuel your actions.

And may connection always call you home.

With gratitude,

Michelle and Dennis Reina

The Art of Trust Building
Discussion Guide

This guide is designed to accompany your reading of *The Art of Trust Building* and spark meaningful reflection and conversation—whether you're using it for personal growth, leadership development, or group facilitation.

Introduction

Reflection: How do you currently sense trust in your relationships or work environments? Describe what it feels like when trust is present—and when it's absent.

Discussion: What practices or mindsets help you stay grounded and present in a way that fosters trust?

Chapter One

Reflection: When you consider the journey of trust, where do you naturally begin—with trusting others, or with trusting yourself? What helps you lean into trust, and what makes you pull back? Take a moment to notice your starting line: What strengthens your willingness to trust, and what undermines it?

Discussion: What does it mean to trust yourself—and why is that the foundation for trusting others? How might deepening self-trust expand your capacity to build, extend, and repair trust in your relationships?

Reflection: What belief systems do you hold about trust? Which ones might be limiting you?

Discussion: How do you shift from a fear-based mindset to one rooted in curiosity, compassion, and courage?

Chapter Two

Reflection: When have you seen consistency and integrity modeled powerfully? How did it impact you?

Discussion: What are ways you can build trust through the alignment of your actions and values?

Chapter Three

Reflection: What holds you back from telling the truth in difficult moments?

Discussion: What does "radical honesty with compassion" look like in your context?

Chapter Four

Reflection: Who has believed in your capability before you believed in yourself? How did that shape your growth?

Discussion: How can you more intentionally support others' growth and decision-making?

Chapter Five

Reflection: What small choices did you make this week that either built or eroded trust?

Discussion: How do you stay mindful of trust building as a practice, not a destination?

Chapter Six

Reflection: Think of a moment where trust was broken. What could have helped prevent the broken trust or rebuild the lost trust?

Discussion: What does taking responsibility look like without shame or blame?

Chapter Seven

Reflection: Reflect on a moment when someone's trust in you sparked something bigger—something beyond the immediate relationship. Which of the four characteristics—courage, compassion, community, or conviction—were present? Which do you want to more intentionally bring into your way of being?

Discussion: What is your conviction when it comes to relationships? What do you believe in so deeply that it shapes how you show up, even when it's hard? How might that conviction guide you to deepen your presence and cultivate trust more intentionally in the spaces you influence?

Chapter Eight

Reflection: Think of a time when you offered or received gratitude that changed the tone of a relationship. What made it meaningful? How did it expand trust in yourself and in others?

Discussion: What is your conviction about honoring others? How can you transform gratitude from a passing expression into a consistent way of being—one that communicates "you matter" not just with words, but through trust building presence, support, and acknowledgment?

Conclusion

Reflection: After engaging with this book, what have you become more aware of in how you trust yourself—and how you extend or withhold trust from others? What shifts are you noticing in your mindset, your habits, or your presence?

Discussion: What commitments are you taking forward to deepen trust in your relationships, teams, or communities?

Notes

Preface

1   Reina, Dennis S. "The Impact of Touch on Trust within Work Teams Using Experiential Learning Methodology." PhD diss., Fielding Graduate University, Santa Barbara, 1995; Chagnon, Michelle Lorraine. "The Impact of Boundary Management across the Organizational System." PhD diss., Fielding Graduate University, Santa Barbara, 1997; Reina, Dennis S., and Reina, Michelle L. *Trust and Betrayal in the Workplace: Building Effective Relationships in Your Organization.* 1st ed. San Francisco: Berrett-Koehler, 1999.

2   Reina, Dennis. S, and Reina, Michelle. L. *Reina Individual Trust Scale*® Assessment. Stowe, VT: Reina Trust Building, 2025.

Introduction

1   Reina, Dennis S., and Reina, Michelle L. *Trust and Betrayal in the Workplace: Building Effective Relationships in Your Organization.* 1st, 2nd, and 3rd eds. San Francisco: Berrett-Koehler, 1999, 2006, 2015.

2   Reina, Dennis S., and Reina, Michelle L. *Rebuilding Trust in the Workplace: Seven Steps to Renew Confidence, Commitment, and Energy.* Oakland: Berrett-Koehler, 2010.

3   Reina, Dennis S., and Reina, Michelle L. *The Seven Steps for Healing.* Oakland: Berrett-Koehler, 2010.

Chapter 1

1   Reina, Dennis S., and Reina, Michelle L. "Capacity for Trust." In
    Trust and Betrayal in the Workplace. Oakland: Berrett-Koehler,
    1999, 2006, 2015.

Chapter 2

1   Reina, Dennis S., and Reina, Michelle L. "Trust of Character." In
    Trust and Betrayal in the Workplace. Oakland: Berrett-Koehler,
    1999, 2006, 2015.

Chapter 3

1   Reina, Dennis S., and Reina, Michelle L. "Trust of Communication."
    In *Trust and Betrayal in the Workplace*. Oakland: Berrett-Koehler,
    1999, 2006, 2015.
2   Angelou, Maya quote: "Forgive yourself for not knowing what
    you didn't know before you learned it." From her writings on self-
    compassion and forgiveness.
3   Reina, Dennis S., and Reina, Michelle L. *Rebuilding Trust in the
    Workplace: Seven Steps to Renew Confidence, Commitment, and
    Energy*. Oakland: Berrett-Koehler, 2010.

Chapter 4

1   Reina, Dennis S., and Reina, Michelle L. "Trust of Capability."
    In *Trust and Betrayal in the Workplace*. Oakland: Berrett-Koehler,
    1999, 2006, 2015.
2   Reina, Dennis S., and Reina, Michelle L. "Three Dimensions of
    Trust: The Three Cs." In *Trust and Betrayal in the Workplace*.
    Oakland: Berrett-Koehler, 1999, 2006, 2015.

Chapter 5

1   Reina, Dennis S., and Reina, Michelle L. *Rebuilding Trust in the
    Workplace: Seven Steps to Renew Confidence, Commitment, and
    Energy*. Oakland: Berrett-Koehler, 2010.

Chapter 6

1   Walia, Ana. "'If It's a Comedy, Fall Over It': Michael Caine Could Not Believe the Advice He Got after a Chair Got Stuck on a Door." Animated Times, September 24, 2023. *https://animatedtimes.com /if-its-a-comedy-fall-over-it-michael-caine-could-not-believe-the -advice-he-got-after-a-chair-got-stuck-on-a-door/.*

2   Reina, Dennis S., and Reina, Michelle L. *Rebuilding Trust in the Workplace: Seven Steps to Renew Confidence, Commitment, and Energy.* Oakland: Berrett-Koehler, 2010.

Chapter 7

1   Reina, Dennis S., and Reina, Michelle L. "Transformative Trus." In *Trust and Betrayal in the Workplace.* Oakland: Berrett-Koehler, 1999, 2006, 2015.

2   Mandela, N. *Long Walk to Freedom: The Autobiography of Nelson Mandela.* New York: Little, Brown and Company, 1994.

3   Vickery, Lou, and Smith, Sonny. *Winning the "Head" Game: Key to Elite Athletic Status.* C2C Publishing, 2021.

4   Hildebrand, Laura. *Unbroken: A World War II Story of Survival, Resilience and Redemption.* New York: Random House, 2010.

5   Dalai Lama and Cutler, H. C. *The Art of Happiness: A Handbook for Living.* New York: Riverhead Books, 1998.

6   Moses, Martin. "Jacqueline Kiplimo: When Kenyan Athlete Helped Athlete with Disability Drink Water." *MSN*, August 26, 2024. *https:// www.tuko.co.ke/sports/athletics/559963-jacqueline-kiplimo-kenyan -athlete-helped-athlete-disability-drink-water/.*

Chapter 8

1   Martela, F., and Nandram, S. "Buurtzorg: Scaling Up an Organization with Hundreds of Self-Managing Teams but No Middle Managers." *Journal of Organization Design.* (2025).

2   Kelly, J. "Gen-Z's Are Redefining the Way They Want to Work." *Forbes*, April 2025. *https://www.forbes.com/sites/jackkelly/2025 /04/01/gen-zs-takeover-and-redefining-the-workplace/.*

3   Emmons, Robert A. *Thanks! How the New Science of Gratitude Can Make You Happier.* Boston: Houghton Mifflin. 2007.

Resources

REINA INDIVIDUAL TRUST SCALE ASSESSMENT

Build Self-Awareness. Strengthen Relationships. Inspire Trust.

Discover how you build—or unintentionally break—trust with the Reina Individual Trust Scale Assessment. This research-based self-report tool gives you a clear, actionable snapshot of your trustworthiness, helping you

- gain insight into how your behaviors impact trust in your relationships;
- recognize strengths and identify opportunities to enhance your effectiveness; and
- apply personalized coaching tips and action plans grounded in decades of trust building expertise.

The assessment measures your self-perceived trustworthiness through the lens of everyday behaviors, those that build trust and those that erode it. Responses are gathered using a five-point Likert scale, offering a nuanced view of how you currently show up in relationships at work and in life.

Your trustworthiness is one of your greatest leadership assets.

When people trust you, they collaborate more openly, communicate more honestly, and rely on you in times of uncertainty. Trust isn't just a feel-good value; it's the foundation of high-performing relationships and thriving teams.

Learn how to strengthen it. Complete the Reina Individual Trust Scale Assessment and unlock your personalized insights report with practical, expert-backed coaching guidance to support your trust building journey.

reinatrustbuilding.com/ITS-book

Acknowledgments

To our publishing partner, Berrett-Koehler: Our relationship with Berrett-Koehler spans over twenty-seven years—a testament to the power of trusting relationships that last. We are so grateful to walk this path with you.

- Steve Piersanti, founder and CEO, and our editor—thank you for embracing the vision of this book from the start. Your guidance, insightful questions, and steady encouragement stretched us and supported us in bringing this work fully into form.

- Kristen Frantz, dear friend and longtime adviser—thank you for your belief that *this* was the book that needed to be written and written now. Your conviction was a guiding light.

- Jeevan Sivasubramanian, thank you for your consistent reminder to stay grounded in what matters most.

We are grateful to the reviewers of early manuscript drafts. Your thoughtful feedback helped us see how to refine this work and shape it into the book it was meant to become. Thank you, Tora Estep, Erik Rasmussen, Tim Rauen, Candace Sinclair, and Jim Wylde.

Tim Shields, thank you for your creative insight and fresh perspective. Your contributions helped us reshape and rearticulate core concepts throughout this book with clarity and resonance.

To our team at Reina Trust Building:

- Amanda Fallon, Jen Colmenero, and Olivia Winslow, thank you for overseeing the day-to-day service of our clients with wisdom and care, making it possible for us to devote ourselves to this writing.

- Jenn Beverage, thank you for your thoughtful design insight and intuitive approach, making it smooth and seamless for us to orient this book's message to reach every person—at every level—within an organization. You help us reach the heart of the business where trust truly lives, and you do it with heart, insight, and joy.

- Melanie Martinelli, thank you for helping to serve clients globally, extending the essence of trust to people and cultures worldwide.

- Katherine Armstrong, we are grateful for your wholehearted dedication to serving clients through your powerful facilitation, demonstrated actions, insightful guidance, and impactful executive coaching.

- Jon Michelson, your powerful analysis into our trust assessments has helped illuminate where individuals, leaders, and teams can use this book as a tool for action.

- Bob von Elgg, our graphic designer of the models that gave visual form to the Trust Building framework, bringing it to life in a practical and applicable way. Thank you.

We are grateful to our Reina Master Practitioners, whose ongoing dedication to teaching and living the principles of Trust Building spreads this work across the globe, making a lasting difference. Thank you, Sam Kurian, TC Yeo, David Lim, David Hudnut, Jawad Ahmed, and Dr. Mohammad Algarni. Your partnership, presence, and belief in this work continue to make a lasting difference.

In our broader circle of life, we are blessed by the presence of collaborators and friends whose unique gifts have enriched this work in meaningful ways:

- Dr. Cynda Rushton, thank you for your collaboration in bringing trust building into the fabric of healthcare systems—especially in support of nurses who serve at the heart of humanity. We are never done . . . yet we are always in process.

- Davida Sharpe, thank you for helping us create powerful, transformative learning experiences for our clients to grow from.

- Gladys Ortiz, thank you for your dedication to teaching leaders and teams how to bring trust building into their lives—and for showing them how it's done by how you live it.

- Sharon Ryan, thank you for infusing trust building into organizations across four continents over the past twenty years. You've carried the torch with unwavering heart, and your impact continues to ripple far and wide.

- Yolanda Conyers, what began as a relationship with Michelle, through executive coaching, has grown into a treasured friendship. Your continual support, thoughtful insight, and courageous leadership have profoundly influenced how we bring trust building to leaders around the world.

- Paul Chagnon—Michelle's brother and a rock solid individual in our lives. Thank you for always being there when we need you, with steady presence, strength, and love. Your support means more than words can say.

- And, finally to the individuals, leaders, teams, and organizations who have given us the privilege of serving them.

To each person named here—and to the many others who have touched this journey in quiet, meaningful ways—we offer our deepest thanks. Your presence, belief, and generosity of spirit have helped bring this book to life. We carry your support with us, and it lives in every page. This work reflects the trust we've shared, and we are honored to walk this path with you.

With gratitude,
Michelle and Dennis

Index

About the Authors

Dennis and Michelle Reina—
A Lifelong Journey in Trust Building

Drs. Dennis and Michelle Reina are internationally recognized pioneers in the field of organizational trust. As cofounders of **Reina Trust Building**, they've devoted their lives to helping people build trust that lasts—bringing heart, science, and practical wisdom to workplaces around the world.

Their work has reached countless leaders and teams through their bestselling books, including *Trust and Betrayal in the Workplace: Building Effective Relationships in Your Organization* (in its third edition) and *Rebuilding Trust in the Workplace: Seven Steps to Renew Confidence, Commitment, and Energy*. But for Dennis and Michelle, this journey goes far beyond the pages of a book—it's deeply personal.

Growing up in military families, both Dennis and Michelle learned early on how much relationships matter—whether navigating change, adapting to new environments, or relying on others under pressure. From those early life lessons to climbing rock faces in Yosemite and working across cultures and industries worldwide, they came to understand that **trust is the glue** that holds people and performance together.

Dennis and Michelle met in graduate school, where they discovered a shared passion for making trust practical in everyday work and life. That passion became their mission. In 1991, they began consulting together, focusing on building self-directed work teams and fixing failed change efforts. At the time, few people recognized how important trust was for these goals—and even fewer offered clear guidance on how to build or rebuild it. So, Dennis and Michelle set out to fill that gap. They conducted post-doctoral research into trust building and used what they learned to help organizations around the world create high-performing, trust-based cultures.

They launched **Reina Trust Building** with a vision: to transform the way people work and live together by strengthening trust at every level. What makes the Reinas' work so impactful is how they've taken trust—something that often feels abstract or intangible—and turned it into something people can *see, measure, and practice.* Their simple yet powerful frameworks help leaders and teams build, rebuild, and sustain trust through clear, intentional behaviors. These tools are used by Fortune 500 companies, healthcare systems, government agencies, and nonprofits around the world to embed trust into their cultures.

Today, Dennis and Michelle are not only respected authorities, authors, and speakers—they're trusted trust building guides. They've supported thousands of leaders in navigating the real challenges of trust: how to grow it, how to protect it, and how to repair it when it breaks. They don't just teach trust—they live it.

For them, trust building is more than a profession. It's a purpose. A passion. And every time someone shares how their work has led to deeper relationships, stronger teams, or personal transformation, Dennis and Michelle are reminded why they do what they do.

Trust building, after all, is at the heart of everything that works.

Working with Reina Trust Building

Trust building work begins with a choice.

Reina Trust Building exists for one powerful reason: to build cultures of trusting relationships that heal, connect, and empower people to grow and collaborate so they thrive—*together*. For thirty-five years, that mission has guided everything Reina does—from how they partner with clients to how they support teams, leaders, and entire organizations through change, challenge, and growth.

The firm focuses a human-centered approach on the use and application of trust research and processes, assessments, and learning tools in the workplace. Drawing on vast experience from working across industries and cultures, Reina Trust Building offers practical tools that help people build and rebuild trust in concrete, measurable ways.

Behind every successful organization is a network of strong relationships.

When trust is present, people collaborate better, communicate more openly, and perform at higher levels. When trust is lacking, even the most carefully crafted strategies can falter.

Our best-in-class, statistically valid, and reliable assessments set the industry standard for measuring trust. Learn more about capturing actionable data around the trust of leaders, teams, and organizations. reinatrustbuilding.com/assessments

Working together builds mutual trust and respect.

Reina makes trust real and practical, translating trust from a concept to a reality by clearly defining the observable, measurable behaviors that make or break trust. It emphasizes the personal responsibility to be trustworthy and the conscious decision to extend trust to others. These choices bring clarity and give people a shared language for talking about trust.

> *Learn more about how to help people understand the behaviors that make or break trust with our proven, research-based programs, tools, and resources.*
> *reinatrustbuilding.com/services*

Trust transforms cultures.

Reina's integrated ecosystem supports transformation at every level of the organization. If your goal is to transform individual leaders, teams, or scale impact throughout your organization to build a culture of trust, Reina's solutions lead to higher engagement, satisfaction, and productivity.

> **Assessments:** *Reina Leadership Trust Scale® • Reina Team Trust Scale® • Reina Organizational Trust Scale® • Reina Customer Trust Scale®*

> **Programs:** *Offer a place to engage, connect, and apply trust building in real time with our suite of Trust Building® and Seven Steps for Healing® learning experiences.*

> **Certifications:** *Scale Reina's assessment and program solutions.*

> **Coaching:** *Support leaders to deepen consistency and credibility while accelerating impact.*

> **Consulting:** *Build trust into the fabric of essential systems and strategies, especially during times of change and transformation.*

Learn more about Reina Trust Building®

> *reinatrustbuilding.com*

Berrett-Koehler
PUBLISHERS

Berrett-Koehler is an independent publisher dedicated to an ambitious mission: *Connecting people and ideas to create a world that works for all.*

Our publications span many formats, including print, digital, audio, and video. We also offer online resources, training, and gatherings. And we will continue expanding our products and services to advance our mission.

We believe that the solutions to the world's problems will come from all of us, working at all levels: in our society, in our organizations, and in our own lives. Our publications and resources offer pathways to creating a more just, equitable, and sustainable society. They help people make their organizations more humane, democratic, diverse, and effective (and we don't think there's any contradiction there). And they guide people in creating positive change in their own lives and aligning their personal practices with their aspirations for a better world.

And we strive to practice what we preach through what we call "The BK Way." At the core of this approach is *stewardship*, a deep sense of responsibility to administer the company for the benefit of all of our stakeholder groups, including authors, customers, employees, investors, service providers, sales partners, and the communities and environment around us. Everything we do is built around stewardship and our other core values of *quality, partnership, inclusion,* and *sustainability.*

We are grateful to our readers, authors, and other friends who are supporting our mission. We ask you to share with us examples of how BK publications and resources are making a difference in your lives, organizations, and communities at bkconnection.com/impact.

Dear reader,

Thank you for picking up this book and welcome to the worldwide BK community! You're joining a special group of people who have come together to create positive change in their lives, organizations, and communities.

What's BK all about?

Our mission is to connect people and ideas to create a world that works for all.

Why? Our communities, organizations, and lives get bogged down by old paradigms of self-interest, exclusion, hierarchy, and privilege. But we believe that can change. That's why we seek the leading experts on these challenges—and share their actionable ideas with you.

A welcome gift

To help you get started, we'd like to offer you a free copy of one of our bestselling ebooks:

bkconnection.com/welcome

When you claim your **free ebook**, you'll also be subscribed to our blog.

Our freshest insights

Access the best new tools and ideas for leaders at all levels on our blog at ideas.bkconnection.com.

Sincerely,
Your friends at Berrett-Koehler